MARATHON
mum

MARATHON
mum

How one woman's fight for mental health inspired a running revolution

by

RACHEL BROWN with WARREN FITZGERALD

AD LIB

First published in 2021 by Ad Lib Publishers Ltd
15 Church Road
London, SW13 9HE
www.adlibpublishers.com

Text © 2021 Rachel Brown with Warren FitzGerald

Paperback ISBN 978-1-913543-66-2
eBook ISBN 978-1-913543-65-5

A CIP catalogue record for this book is available from the
British Library.
Every reasonable effort has been made to trace copyright-
holders of material reproduced in this book, but if any have
been inadvertently overlooked the publishers would be glad to
hear from them.

Printed in the UK
10 9 8 7 6 5 4 3 2 1

For Dad, my hero

1

SUNSET OVER BIRKENHEAD

We've been hiking up Kilimanjaro for five days now. The rust-bucket bus squeaked and shuddered its way from the hotel in Dar es Salaam eighteen hundred feet up to base camp, then left us to do the rest on foot. It's the only way you can get to the top of such a big bloody mountain, of course. And I can't think of a better way to get over this latest obstacle in my life.

On foot.

These feet of mine have already carried me such a long way. They've helped me leg it from the bullies back in school, they've danced me from the murky waters of the Mersey to the bright lights of the Far East, they've scarpered across departure lounges and car parks and down hospital corridors, freed me from psychotic controlling husbands, carried me across finish lines and crossed the paths of women who changed my life forever, and who tell me I've changed theirs, and – I'm not blowing my own trumpet here when I say – they are feet that have raised thousands of pounds for great causes. And feet which once rushed me back from Hong Kong too late, *too late* to save the one person I loved more than anyone else in this world.

'Washey, washey!'

That's Moses. He's one of twenty Tanzanian guides our group of thirty have got on this trek and he means it's time for our daily bath. Or, in other words, our daily crouch at one of the bowls of steaming hot water they've boiled for us to wash our hands and faces in with some Dettol soap.

We couldn't have done all this without these guides in their flip-flops and jeans, too small for them, and their Manchester United T-shirts, too big for them, which all the African lads seem to wear, while we go up in full mountaineering kit: the boots, the layers of luminous wet weather gear. We fart about with our little day packs while they climb the same enormous mountain with our luggage on their heads, or Portaloos on their backs, and buckets of raw chicken in their hands ready to cook for our tea.

'We have to sort out their clothes for them,' Clare, one of my besties, had said on the first day.

Then one of our group sighed, 'Yeah, poor sods, they're going to be cold tonight, surely.'

'Sod that,' Clare said. 'I mean, we have to swap those Manchester United shirts for Liverpool ones.'

Every day the guides would steam ahead and, by the time we staggered into the next camp, they'd have all our tents set up for us with a big tarpaulin spread over the dusty earth and all our bags set out on it. They'd do us a lovely snack of warm salty popcorn and ginger biscuits, then comes:

'Washey, Washey!'

As we start to wash, Clare says under her breath, 'We should get the African boys to have a go at this too, shouldn't we? They don't half pong some of them.'

Clare's obsessively clean and tidy. By the time I've finished washing, she'll have all our gear laid out in neat rows on our sleeping bags in the tent.

'Get that down you,' I say to her handing her a tin mug of tea. 'I know what you mean, though. Isn't it funny how they have that certain... aroma about them and we don't? Especially since we haven't had a proper wash in days.'

As we gossip about BO we start to undress, stripping off more layers than usual since the weather is surprisingly warm today.

'Oh my God!' we say in sync as we realise that under all those body suits and fleeces we smell exactly the same as our lovely guides. We laugh like a couple of schoolgirls – we've gone hysterical up here in the thin air; everything seems funnier the more extreme the situation gets.

We've chosen the seven-day trek as opposed to the five day. If you take the five-day one you're more likely to suffer from altitude sickness, we've been told. Our seven-day one means, although we spend most of the time trekking *up* the mountain, which is let's face it the best direction to go in if you want to get to the top of anything, we come down a little bit each night to sleep as that helps with any sickness. I've had a headache every day, but that's about it. Other people have been honking up left, right and centre. Lee is suffering terribly with his blood pressure, and Paul has gone blind – temporarily we're told. They call it snow blindness, something to do with the altitude. We have a doctor with us who says they'll be all right, but it looks like they won't make it to the top. We're all dead worried about them, and if I'm honest, I'm petrified something like that'll happen to me. I'd be gutted beyond belief if I didn't make it to the top. I have to make it to the top. For the kids, for myself. For my mental health.

Before I try to sleep I go out to watch the sunset – a red disc which you just don't get over Birkenhead – burning its way through the clouds below us. Below us! Yes, we're so high that the world has turned upside down. It makes me sob and smile all at the same time, this view. Look how far I've come! And I'm not talking about Kilimanjaro. Well, not just, anyway. Being up here looking down like this is like being in a plane only better.

And suddenly I'm back inside a plane going from Hong Kong to London. A plane journey that felt like it would never end. A plane journey I couldn't wait to be over, because I needed to be back home yesterday.

It's twenty-seven years earlier, 1989, and I'm dancing in Hong Kong at the time. I'm a professional dancer. I'd wanted to be a dancer since I was a little girl. It was my dream. But alongside the dream were nightmares. Night terrors when I was convinced I was going to die and my main worry about dying, even then, was that I was going to snuff it before I had a chance to do something amazing, something that people would remember me for. I decided from a very young age that the way I would achieve this would be by being the next Bette Midler. So I didn't need to worry about studying at school because I was, without doubt, going to be an actress and a singer. The only trouble was I had a severe stammer and the bullies loved that. They took the piss out of me all the way through school, primary and secondary, so I needed to find somewhere else, away from school, where I could work on bringing out that Hollywood star that was locked away inside me.

The Port Sunlight Players were an amateur dramatics group based in the civic centre close to my town. It was run by an old lady – well, she seemed old to me at the time – and this seventeen-year-old called Brian McCann – dead talented for his years. At the age of fifteen, I joined up and the first play we did was *Equus*. I bagged the part of Jill the stable girl who had to snog the leading man played by my friend's ridiculously hot cousin, Andy. I should have been all over him. I probably would have been in private, but I just couldn't snog him on stage in front of everybody. He looked like Johnny Depp and thank God they cut the naked bit from the play because I wouldn't have known where to look then.

For one of the rehearsals at the Glenda Jackson Theatre I turned up early and Brian, who was directing, was already there tinkling away on the piano. I sat down and listened. He was dead good, playing a Christmas song he'd written for the next show:

'I'm Santa Claus as everyone knows, a fat man with a beard,
I'm dressed in red, silly hat on my head, but no one thinks I'm
weird.'

I gave him a little clap when he'd finished and then told him how worried I was about kissing Andy in front of an audience. He was sympathetic and told me he had an idea. When Andy arrived, he sent us both off to another room to practise the kiss, to get over it, so it wasn't such a big deal. But when the first night of the play came around and I went on stage for the kissing scene, I couldn't concentrate, my mind went blank except for thoughts of snogging this gorgeous boy in front of all these people and I completely fluffed my lines, made a mess of the whole thing and left the Port Sunlight Players in shame as soon as the play was over, thinking I'd let Brian and everyone else down.

So being Bette Midler never really happened as I'd hoped it would. I couldn't sing and it turned out I was crap at acting too. So school became a place where I spent all my time trying to be liked instead. As my end of term reports would say:

'Once Rachel realises she's not here to win a popularity contest we'll get along much better.'

Most of the teachers would look at me with such disappointment and ask me why I couldn't be like our Lynne, my big sister, who always paid attention in class, always did her homework, always looked smart. To this I would stick my finger down my throat and look around to see who was laughing.

The only teacher who didn't have a go at me was Mrs Reed. She looked for the best in every student; unearthed their qualities and nurtured them. She encouraged me to do the Duke of Edinburgh Award, which was all the rage at the time. There was the bronze, the silver, then the gold award. When I was fourteen, about sixty of us started off doing the bronze in my secondary school – Bebington Secondary School for Girls, or Beb Sec, as we called it – and one of the first things we had to do was a camping exercise. The first night of the camp, me and my mates arranged to meet some boys by the river, but we were soon sprung by one of the eagle-eyed teachers, Mrs Kimpton.

'Rachel, if you don't focus, you won't even get through your bronze,' she pleaded with me, 'never mind the silver.'

In my little universe I just thought she was still miffed at me from the time she asked me to babysit her little girl and I decided to take her to the seaside and on the waltzer, which of course she was far too young to be on – she could have slipped out and flown across the pier to a very messy end. Still, she loved every second of it.

'I'll show you,' I sulked as we were all sent back to our damp tents in disgrace.

And so I smashed the bronze, kicked the arse of the silver, and by the time we got to the gold there were only a few of us left who hadn't given up. We had to do the gold at Rock Ferry High School where some boys were doing it too. That was a right laugh. 'If Mrs Kimpton could see me now,' I giggled, as we sneaked off to the pub with the lads for a snog and a beer.

I soon started seeing one of the lads called John. We quickly got serious and we were both invited to Buckingham Palace to receive our gold award from the Duke of Edinburgh himself – me being the only girl from Beb Sec who got her gold.

As Prince Philip approached me and John, our mums looked on, pleased as punch, until the Duke said to me, 'And what did you get out of doing the Duke of Edinburgh Award, young lady?'

'An engagement ring and a fiancé,' I said, elbowing John.

My mum went white, but Philip thought I was 'a hoot'.

Mrs Reed was dead proud of me seeing the scheme through. She'd also encouraged me to follow my passion for performing even when other teachers tried to put me down. OK, I couldn't sing or act. But I could dance. None of your ballet, or tap or anything else that you needed lots of training for, but funky dancing – I suppose what you'd call street dance these days – was something I could do naturally. Ever since I used to entertain my dad by wobbling about the living room like the girl from the title sequence of *Tales of the Unexpected* as he watched it on the telly, or learning every iota of the moves for Michael Jackson's *Thriller*, dance was something I could do *my* way, and since I was never really good at doing things by the book, it was perfect for me.

The trouble was the drama and dance teacher at school, Mrs Burns, thought otherwise. Mrs Burns thought she was so bohemian, with her floral smocks and long black locks as she strutted round the school, but she just looked like Kate Bush with her face punched in and a rod up her arse. Unlike Mrs Reed, she couldn't see through all my fannying around. She refused to put me in any shows, while she put my mate Karen in everything. Everyone knew me and Karen were two of the best dancers in the school – especially since we'd knocked it out of the park with our routine to *Ghostbusters* at the end of term talent competition – but Mrs Burns never even let on there was an opportunity to study dance in college and she even laughed at me when I danced for an exam.

Even though Mrs Burns tried to shit on my dreams of being a dancer, when I left school me and Karen still managed to get a job in a new club called the Pleasuredrome in Birkenhead. There was seven of us in the dance troupe and all the other girls were trained; they could do a load of moves that I couldn't do and they were dead, dead pretty. I was always more of a tomboy and so I took the role of the clown, you know: if they walked on in their fishnet tights, short military jackets and caps at a sexy angle, I'd walk on in a trench coat and an oversized tin hat, pretending to cock up all the moves. But when it came to dancing, funky dancing, I could really hold my own. Even the female punters would come up to me and say, 'God you're brill, you. You're a wicked dancer and your body's ace. Can you tell us what diet you're on?' It was a far cry from being bullied back in school. It did my self-esteem and my stammer no end of good.

I still got cab drivers asking me if I was drunk when I tried to call up for a taxi at the end of the night. I still got people yelling, 'Spit it out!' as if I was back in school. I'd look daggers at those who suggested it was my fault, as if, before I was born, I spotted the queue for stammerers, thought 'I'll have a bit of that,' and got in line. But then there were people like Matt, this Aussie guy, who caught me on my way out the club one night.

'You're not different, you know.' He smiled a big white smile.

I wondered where this was going and was prepared to give him a mouthful when he went on:

'You're unique. And don't let anyone tell you any different. Even that stammer. Every stammerer has their own unique stammer. As unique as a fingerprint. They laugh,' he said, nodding to the bar where some dickhead had done just that at me earlier, 'but we have to be understanding and forgive them. They don't get it. They don't get that it only comes out like that because you fear it coming out like that. But don't you give a shit about it. Coz the less you care, the less it'll happen.'

He must have been a stammerer too, though there was no sign of it when he spoke. But that was just it. He probably didn't give a shit. And the more my confidence was boosted by dancing, the less of a shit I gave too. I had such a good time at the Pleasuredrome, it was such a popular place and us dancers soon became famous... well, famous in Birkenhead.

'Ey, look who's in the audience!' Karen said to me out the corner of her mouth one night as we sashayed round the stage.

'Who?' I hissed back.

'Mrs Burns.'

'Never.'

'Let's go over and say hello,' Karen said when we'd finished our routine.

I wasn't exactly dying to reminisce about the good old days with Mrs Bloody Burns but I went over with Karen anyway, and instead of the cold shoulder I was expecting, Mrs Burns was all over us. She almost seemed a bit star struck. She put on her best scouse accent to try and show she was one of us and said, 'Oh my God, you was dead good. And just think, I made yers.'

'Er… no,' I said looking her square in the eye. 'You didn't make me.' And I turned round and strutted away harder than she ever could, leaving her jaw on the floor of the club among the fag ends and the spilt beer.

The other girls in the group would tell me about auditions they were going to at Pineapple Dance Studios in London. Auditions where two hundred girls turned up for a cruise ship or hotel job that only required six dancers. And the first thing they'd ask you to do would be triple time steps and bombershay with a paradiddle-piddle-piss-bollocks whatever it was and, of course, I didn't have the foggiest what they were talking about, so I'd be out before I'd even warmed up. And I'd sit there watching my mates get down to the final twenty and then they'd ask them to do all the jazz and funk dancing, the stuff that they would be doing in the actual shows, and I'd be thinking, 'I can do that standing on my head.' So I ended up taking my ghetto blaster down to a talent agency in Manchester and I said to them, 'Look, I can do what you need us to do on the cruise ship shows, but I just can't do all

that stuff you make us do at the beginning of the auditions.'
So I danced in front of a little panel of agents there as if I was
that girl out of *Flashdance* and they offered me a job in Hong
Kong. Hong bloody Kong! I was going to be dancing abroad
in a proper top class theatre. Two shows a night, Equity
contract, the lot. But I was only nineteen at the time, living at
home in our little semi in sleepy Bebington and I thought my
dad might tell me it was too much, too soon, too far.

In fact, when I told him I'd be travelling halfway across
the globe to go and dance, he had no bother with it at all.

'Superb!' he said.

He couldn't wait for me to go and see the world. He'd
been in the merchant navy and sailed all over the place.
He'd had the time of his life doing that and he wanted me
to experience it too. He called up the agent first though. He
checked it all out and then, when he was sure, he said he was
more than happy for me to go. Down the pub he told all his
mates that his daughter was going abroad as a professional
dancer. Proud as a peacock, he was.

He took me and Karen, who also got the job, up to
Manchester when the time came, so we could get our flight
down to London because from there we'd be flying to Hong
Kong to rehearse for a month before the shows. But Karen's
mum, who'd booked the flights, cocked up and told us to get
to the airport an hour later than we should have so when
we got there the gate was closing and we were about to miss
our connection to London. All hell broke loose and we were
begging the check-in staff, 'Please, please, just let us through.
We'll leg it straight to the gate, we'll even leave our luggage
behind, whatever it takes, just let us go!'

'No, I'm sorry, madam,' this dolly bird behind the counter
said, 'you'll have to wait for the next flight.'

She was really getting on my nerves until she told us the next flight was so soon after the one we'd missed, that she could radio London and tell the Hong Kong flight to wait for us – now I wanted to kiss her. But when Karen and I finally got through security, instead of rushing off to the departure gate I turned to see my dad standing there waving us goodbye. I waved back. And he kept on waving. He waved and he waved, and I waved and waved, until...

'Hurry up, Rach!' Karen hissed tugging at my sleeve.

We had to go through to the gates. Only then did I lose sight of Dad, but for all I knew he was still waving, bless him.

When we got to London and they asked us for our passports to get on the international flight, Karen realised she'd left hers with her mum, so we couldn't get on the flight after all. We had to stay in a hotel overnight in Heathrow and catch another flight the next day. We called the manager of the dance troupe in Hong Kong, told him what was happening and he went spare down the phone at us, while Karen's boyfriend drove down that night to London with the missing passport. And if we hadn't had enough grief already, when we went to pick up our luggage from the carousel, as we were told to do by the airline staff, it had disappeared. All my new make-up and all my new clothes, gone. I never did find out what happened to it. Something was trying to stop us from going to Hong Kong that day, I swear.

But we made it eventually. Karen and I were squealing as our plane came in to land between all the Oriental, neon high-rises. It was like being in a movie, a science fiction one. We'd never seen anything like it. We spent the first couple of weeks walking round with our gobs hanging open, not looking where we were going because our eyes were always looking up at this sparkling city towering over us. In the bars and restaurants the locals couldn't understand a word we were saying so we had a right laugh making that universal sign for the bill but shouting across the room, 'Can we have the elephant's penis please?' to which the Chinese waiter would smile and nod enthusiastically. Like a couple of bloody schoolkids we were. Having the best time. But while my head was chocka with all these new experiences, I couldn't stop talking about my dad, apparently.

'You don't half talk about him a lot,' Karen said one night as we were getting ready to go out for my birthday.

'I know I do,' I said, 'and I don't know why. Why I don't talk about my mum, I mean, coz I love her just as much.'

Karen had lost her dad many years before and so I'd never met him. We got talking about him and she said when he died she went to see him lying in his coffin in the chapel of rest and it messed with her head. 'Whatever you do, never ever go and see your dad in his coffin,' she warned me.

I just burst out crying at that and said, 'I don't know what I'd do if something happened to my dad, like.'

Anyway, I pulled myself together, reapplied my mascara and we all went down to the harbour that night where we'd hired a boat to party on.

I have no idea what time it was when we finally collapsed into our beds in the hotel, but I was woken in the early hours by the phone ringing and my dad's bestie Bob was on the end of the line saying, 'Rachel, love, you've got to come home, your dad's not well.'

I threw the phone across the floor as I jumped out of bed. All those obstacles we'd had trying to get here in the first place, me talking about my dad all the time, it all suddenly seemed to be a sign; a sign that I should have taken more notice of. And within ten minutes our choreographer was at the door, God love her, trying to get me on a flight. But there was none until the next morning, so she spent the night walking with me around the streets of Hong Kong because there was no way I was going to get to sleep again in the state I was in. All those towers of neon that had sparkled for me for the last few weeks were just a watery blur now through my tears.

Until I got on that flight to London. Then I went out like a light, I was so knackered, and I didn't wake up until the moment we landed and the passengers were all being told to stay seated, 'Except for Rachel Brown, would she please make her way off the aircraft immediately.' I stood up and moved through the cabin like I was still asleep with all these passengers' eyes on me. Maybe they were wondering what I'd done to be ordered off the plane first, or just pissed off that I got to get off before they did perhaps. It was surreal, and so was coming out from that jet bridge to be met by Bob who rushed me to the ozzie telling me Dad had had to have an operation, a routine operation, and he'd said to Mum, 'Don't tell our Rachel coz she'd only worry, like, and she should be enjoying herself while she's away. I'll tell her when she gets back.' But it turned out the surgeon had nipped his bowel during the operation. He'd sewn Dad up again, but the bowel had ruptured after he was back on the ward and septicaemia had set in. Dad had been telling the nurses something wasn't right and they had just said, 'Don't worry, Mr Brown, you just need some painkillers.'

'No,' he told them, 'there's something burst inside of me, there's something burst inside of me.'

For two weeks he was laid up in intensive care. Sedated most of the time. I got there after the first week and I never left his bedside. I spoke to him all the time, so he knew we were there, so he knew he wasn't alone. I would tell him what I'd been doing on my travels. And reminisce about the old days:

'Remember when I was little, Dad? From about the age of three or four, every Saturday night I would sleep with you? Mum would go in our bunk bed with our Lynne, and you would have had a few down the pub and fallen on the magnetic bush. "Well, it must be magnetic, coz it always pulls me in, like," you'd say and wink as you'd stagger in and sit down to your steak and chips. And when you'd polished that off, you'd clap your hands together and say, "Bedtime!" And I couldn't wait, could I. Remember that, Dad? We'd get into bed and read the Ladybird books, *The Three Billy Goats Gruff* or *The Fox and the Gingerbread Man* and I would lie there in exactly the same position every Saturday, my legs over you, like you was a giant pouffe and you'd listen to me read. And when I was done, you'd grin and say, "Nice one! Now, back to back." And we'd get all cosy under the blankets, wouldn't we, back to back and sleep as sound as anything. Perhaps Mum only let me do that so she didn't have to listen to you snoring drunkenly every Saturday night, ey? But I didn't mind, it was our special time. Until I was eleven. Then just before I went to my secondary school, you told me that we weren't going to do our Saturday night sleepovers anymore. I was broken hearted. I couldn't understand why. Of course, I realise why now. You couldn't exactly go to school as an adolescent girl bragging, "I slept with my dad on Saturday night," could you.'

When I went in the hospital shop one day, what did I see there but that Ladybird book *The Three Billy Goats Gruff*. So I bought it like a shot and I read it to Dad as he lay in the hospital bed, just as I used to when I was little. Except this time he had wires going in and out of him and there were monitors going beep all around us. And this time he never said, 'Nice one!' or 'Superb!' He just lay there sleeping.

And he never woke up, ever again.

2

OKAYAMA DREAMS

Perched up there on the edge of Kilimanjaro above the clouds it all came back to me, as if those mountain winds blowing through me had my life story dissolved in them somehow.

When my dad died I felt that life was shit. That it wasn't worth living. I was angry for a very, very long time after that. At the inquest, his death was deemed to be accidental. Our lawyer told us that it would be possible to make a claim against the hospital and we could win a lot of money in compensation, after a lot of time and a lot more heartache.

'Well, I don't care about the money,' my mum said. 'I just want my husband back and that isn't going to happen, is it, so forget it.'

I didn't feel the same way at the time. Not about the money, but about him not coming back. See, I had this idea, and I know it sounds crazy, but I thought if I wished on every eyelash that fell from my eye and every wishbone from the Sunday roasts, if I wished on the birthday candles I blew out and every shooting star – although they were few and far between in the skies over the Mersey – that my dad would come back to us, then he would. And, of course, it wasn't going to happen, it couldn't happen – could it? – but because I always held out that hope, I was setting myself up for depression, big time.

Mum was off work from the office for a few months wandering from room to room in a trance, catching her breath every time the realisation shot through her again that her partner, the love of her life, was gone. And I stayed at home with her, a fist wrapped around my heart that squeezed every time I thought about my dad, so I never got back to do the show we'd been rehearsing for in Hong Kong.

'You're not to stay home just because of me, sweetheart,' my mum would say. 'You've got to go back dancing.'

'But I'm not just staying home because of you, Mum. I *need* to be here with you. I need *you* right now as much as you need me.'

Being around her enabled us both to do everyday things, boring things, like housework or shopping. Things which needed to be done, although neither of us really knew why we were doing them anymore. What was the point if it all ends in pain in a hospital bed? I hated the way we did those things anyway, on autopilot, so I would smoke a lot more instead and take ages to ever start doing them. And if we talked about anything else other than Dad, if we had a laugh about something, I would feel dead guilty about it and terrified that I might be forgetting him.

Then the phone rang one day asking me to come and dance in Singapore with a troupe called Body Talk. I would be dancing in the plush Neptune theatre where Tiffany (as in *I Think We're Alone Now*) and Cliff Richard (as in Number 1 every Christmas for eternity) were singing, so, to me, it really was top notch, a proper opportunity. I called the agent back.

That's when they told me we'd have to do the two opening numbers topless. I was gutted.

'No chance,' I said. 'No wonder they're called Body Talk! There's no way my body'll be talking like that.'

However, the agent went on to explain that these topless dances were going to be the kind of routines the showgirls do in Las Vegas, with strass and feathers cascading down all over your chest from this wonderful bejewelled headgear, so I wouldn't be there just waving my tits around like a lap dancer. No, this was going to be tasteful. But I couldn't stop thinking about what my dad would say. I kept having visions of me on my first night on stage in Singapore, standing there tastefully covered in feathers and rhinestones, just as the agent had said, holding this giant white feather fan high over my head, and there would be the spirit of my dad, somewhere up in the dress circle, looking down through his fingers in horror at his precious daughter standing there with her tits out.

I told my mum and she said, 'You go topless when you go on the beach, sweetheart, so what's the difference?'

'Quite a bit of difference, Mum,' I whined.

'Well, if you've got it…' she smiled. 'Look, you have to go. Your dad was so proud of your dancing. He'd be so upset if you didn't do this.'

The only good reason I could think of to do anything was for my dad. I had always wanted him to be proud of me. Now he was gone – which I still couldn't really believe – the only way I could keep the terror of him totally disappearing at bay, was to keep doing things for him, keep making him proud. So I went.

From Singapore, I danced my way round the rest of Asia, then Europe. Doing what I loved was a tonic – a lifeline in fact. And a couple of years later, I ended up in Okayama, Japan. After the shows in the city we'd go to karaoke bars and have a sing-song, a right laugh it was, and as the time passed I felt less and less guilty about having fun since Dad had gone.

It was in one of these bars we met a group of Japanese blokes. One of them was unusually tall to be Japanese. Six foot tall, long curly hair, skinny as hell and dead nervous – looked more Native American than Japanese, but he wasn't. All the other lads were quite boisterous, you know, and we had a good laugh, but I couldn't help feeling sorry for this shy, skinny one, who they all took the piss out of. I was a one for the waifs and strays, as my mum always said, 'Always bringing in the waifs and strays, even when you were at school. You always brought home the kids who had no other friends.' And she was right, all the ones that got the mickey taken out of them for being smelly or dirty I befriended them – but then I knew what it was like to be bullied. And this Japanese lad was the only one who ever brought a little dictionary out with him, bless him, so he could try and communicate better with us English girls.

So I plonked myself down next to him one night and said, 'What's your name then?'

He looked like a deer in the headlights for a second, almost went for his dictionary, but quickly worked out what I was asking beneath my Merseyside accent, which must have sounded even more alien to him than the American English he heard on TV.

'My name is Osakabenomiko Aisakurako,' he said.

'Oh Jesus, that's a bit of a mouthful, isn't it?' I pondered for a moment then said, 'Tell you what, how about I call you... Max?'

'Max?' Osakabenomiko looked more confused than ever, but a little bit like he was enjoying the idea too.

'And what's your name?' One of the other dancers, Sharon, asked his mate.

'Akihiko Takahashi,' said this big friendly panda of a bloke.

Sharon and I looked at each other for a second, grinning, then we said, almost in unison, 'Jimmy it is then!'

So that's how Max became Max and Jimmy became Jimmy. We got chatting and as the months went by, we all made friends. I didn't fancy Max at all, by the way, wasn't interested in anything like that, but after our year was up in Japan I came back to England and found myself missing him.

I'd been offered a contract in Greece next and another dancer I knew was going to Japan, but she didn't really fancy it, so we decided to swap and I was winging my way back to Okayama in no time and before you knew it I was Max's girlfriend.

When the dancing contract was over, I went to stay with him and his big family very close to Hiroshima – you know the place, where that nuclear bomb was dropped in the Second World War. Little did I know what bombs were about to be dropped for me too there, otherwise I would never have gone.

They had this house with nothing around but paddy fields, from where Max ran a construction firm with his brothers. This part of Okayama didn't exactly have the buzz I was used to, but we had a nice time. Fifteen of us in this little house. Apart from one of Max's brothers, they hardly spoke a word of English and my Japanese stretched to *konichiwa* and *arigato* by this time, but we got by. At first we all had to sleep in one room. It was an L-shape where all fifteen of us would roll out our futons at night. Max and I would sleep round the corner of the L, so we felt like we had some privacy, but it was hardly an en suite. We even had a washing line strung up over us where Max's mother dried the clothes. It didn't stop us trying to have a bit of nookie early in the morning though, fumbling away under our duvets until we heard a noise and then we'd pretend to be asleep as Max's mum came round the corner to hang up more washing. It was only after she'd gone again one day that Max pointed out that his duvet was still hitched up over his knees revealing to his mum that his pyjamas were round his ankles. We had a laugh at that. We had a lot of laughs. At first.

And then one day Max said, 'I want to get married.'

'I'd love to marry you,' I said, 'but I couldn't move away from the UK for good. I need to be close to my mum and our Lynne.'

'But you are always travelling,' he said, looking a bit miffed.

'Yeah, but I love travelling coz I always know I'm going home, like.'

'Well, that is OK,' he smiled, 'I would like to live in the UK too.'

So we agreed to go back to England for our wedding, but just as we were leaving Japan he told me that he was already married. Well, I nearly died, of course, but some things often got lost in translation and I soon found out he meant he'd been married before and was now divorced. 'No biggie,' I thought, 'but why hadn't he told me sooner?' Alarm bells should've rung then, now I think about it. But two days later we were married – six bridesmaids, the Rolls, the whole caboodle, lovely church in the village of Port Sunlight: a model village built by the Lever Brothers to accommodate the workers in their soap factory and it looked as pretty as something from a

Pears soap advert too. The church was where my dad was an altar boy when he was a kid, which is one of the reasons why I chose it – not that Dad was particularly religious, it was just something you did back then, like going to Sunday school as me and our Lynne did.

So there I am after the ceremony in my wedding dress, doing *The Birdie Song* with Auntie Mabel, my uncles all falling off their chairs shit-faced – you know, the way a proper wedding should be – when Max tells me he's got to go back to Japan.

'You what?' I snapped.

But he explained he had to go back to tie up his part of the construction business. He owed his brother some money, apparently, so he'd go and pay him off and be back within a couple of weeks. That was in the June.

By the November, he hadn't come back.

But we'd been in touch regularly. Things were taking longer than expected with the business, he told me, so why didn't I come over for a couple of weeks to celebrate our marriage there with his family and then we'd be back home in England for Christmas. That sounded just ace to me so he sent me the tickets and I was all excited for my little holiday in Japan.

Two and half years later and I was still there in Okayama – a hostage in a house in the middle of nowhere.

3

ME AND TOM COLLINS

He was a different bloke. Not the Max I had fallen in love with, not the Max I had married. He was clearly an alcoholic. Somehow, like the divorce, he'd managed to hide that from me so far. Or perhaps it was being married to me that drove him to drink. But seriously, this new Max was dead cold. He hardly spoke to me. He couldn't even look at me. The family I'd had such a laugh getting to know before had totally changed too and it made me wonder whether he had said something to them to turn them against me. They had moved to a new house, all of them. Max and I had a room to ourselves now, upstairs. Well, I say *our* room. He never really came up there and I never really left it. I wasn't allowed anywhere else. Certainly not in the kitchen. That was Grandma's domain and she'd look at me like I was shit on her shoe if I ever went near it. I felt like a prisoner. I would be sitting up there wondering what the hell had happened and I'd hear all these doors slamming as the family piled into cars and went out for dinner somewhere. I'd watch them from the window as they sped off into town leaving me on my own without so much as a 'see you later'. Soon I noticed Max's teenage nieces were wearing my clothes on their little jaunts out, and money started going missing from my purse too. When all the brothers were at work, Max's nieces would talk to me then, but only to get me to drive them into town for shopping. I did it, hoping it would build bridges with them, but all the way in they would sit behind me in the back seat, gossiping about me and even spitting in my hair as I drove. I was humiliated.

I tried to get Max to talk to me, tell me what was wrong. I begged him to come with me back to England, but he said his brother wouldn't let him go until he'd paid this debt off.

'Tell your brother,' I said, 'when we get home you'll start work there and then you'll be able to send him the money.'

But Max just shook his head, and I couldn't go to the brother directly – none of the family would even talk to me.

This debt clearly had to be paid, and the sooner the better as far as I was concerned, so I persuaded Max to let me work in a private school teaching English as a foreign language and every bit of my wages I gave to him to pay his brother off. But after more than six months nothing had changed. So I'd get off the bus after work every night around 9 p.m., pop in the 7-Eleven, buy six cans of that gin cocktail Tom Collins – dead light, not exactly the hard stuff – but by the time I'd got to the house I would have drunk them all just so I could go straight to sleep and didn't have to deal with being there.

I was so angry. Angry with Max, angry with myself and angry with the family and this brother, Hiroshi, boss of the family business, who was holding Max to ransom like this. So one night instead of going straight to sleep, full of Tom Collins, I went down to Hiroshi (luckily he was the brother who knew some English) and gave him what for. Well, it started off as what for then it kind of turned into me begging.

'Look, Hiroshi, if you don't let us go and work this debt off gradually in England our marriage is not going to last. Is that what you want? How the—'

'Rachel,' he stopped me gently. 'What are you talking about?'

'I mean, do you want to see us fail, is that it?'

'No, I mean, what debt are you talking about?'

'The money Max owes to you.'

Hiroshi leant forward over his desk, looking concerned. 'Max owes me nothing.'

It was all a big con. Max had been lying the whole time. I was gobsmacked at first obviously, but then it was Max's turn to get the sharp end of my tongue.

As I began laying into him, he stopped me and said, 'Come, let's go for a drive!'

I was in my pyjamas at the time, but I didn't care, I'd be happy to go and have this out somewhere else without the rest of the family earwigging. So I didn't even get dressed. I jumped in the car and he drove. He took us up this road that wound round a mountain. And when we got to this car park at the viewing point at the top he got out, came round to my side and locked the door. Then he started pushing the car, screaming that he was going to push it over the edge of the cliff with me in it. Saying that he was going to kill himself after. I knew he wasn't actually going to do it. The handbrake was on for a start – the divvy! – and he was such a skinny rip, he would have barely managed it if it was off, but I was scared nevertheless. I'd heard Max's dad had committed suicide at the age of thirty-two, so perhaps it was in his genes. Or perhaps, knowing how hard I took my dad's death, Max was like he was because of the trauma of losing his dad that way. So I believed the threats when they kept coming after that day. I was frightened for both our lives. I started calling home less and less, but when I did call, my mum could hear it in my voice.

'You all right, love?' she'd say.

'Yeah, Mum, I'm fine, you know,' was all I'd say. I didn't want to worry her, when actually I wanted to scream down the phone at her, tell her how low and frightened I was, isolated in a pokey room in a house in the paddy fields of Oka-fucking-yama on the other side of the bleeding world, being spat on and shat on from a great height. Instead I would just hang up the phone and go back to the room, my cell, and start rubbing my knuckles on the rough wooden walls until they bled. My head was so wrecked I thought it was going to explode so abusing my body like that gave me something else to concentrate on, saved me from going mental – although you might say a young woman hanging the washing out on the line and stabbing herself in the forehead with clothes pegs was already a bit mental.

Even though the cat was out of the bag, Max still took all my wages from teaching and, just in case I was about to do a runner, he had my passport now too. I was down to about seven stone with the stress, my head looked like a balloon on the end of my stick of a body, but somehow those lovely nieces still called me fat and ugly. The only place I could find any solace was at the school where I worked.

There were other foreigners teaching English there – Scottish, Canadian, American – but it was getting harder and harder to hide that I was going off my head. Even the students in the classes were starting to notice. I remember this one girl, Kyomi was her name, looking at me like I was mad. But then again, I think I probably was. In the end, I had a bit of a breakdown in the staff room and confided in some of the other foreigners.

'You've got to get out,' Maggie said, the Scottish one.

'I know, but he's got my passport.'

'OK, you can't leave the country, but you can leave that house.'

'And where do I go?' I sobbed.

'You come and stay with me for a bit.'

'And me,' said this other colleague, Moira.

And then this Canadian one, Douglas goes, 'You can crash on my sofa for a while too.'

So I began to hatch this plan with them. I would just get up one day and leave for work as usual, but not come home. Although, how I was going to get out the house with all my stuff without the family getting suspicious, God knows.

The morning came and I had a word with my dad like I always do at the big moments in my life. When I was trekking through jungles in Asia between gigs, or looking up at skyscrapers in Tokyo, I would be saying to him, 'Look, Dad, look through my eyes, look at all this, can you see?' hoping he would still get to know what I was doing, still get to be proud of me. Today though I didn't ask him to look with wonder through my eyes. I asked him for the strength to go. And I asked him to keep a look out as I stuffed my shoulder bag full of knickers and tops and whatever else I could get in there and still get away with calling it a particularly big pile of books that needed marking.

Max had gone to work already. I had watched him go through quivering eyelashes as I pretended to be sleeping. And before he stirred I had looked at his back, that skinny back of his with his spine showing through, a back that I once loved, like all of him, probably still did, and I cried quietly wondering where it had all gone wrong. This was still on my mind as I zipped up my bag, but now the grief turned to rage. There were a few tops that I'd particularly wanted to take with me but I couldn't find them. That was because they'd been robbed, like so much of my stuff, by those bloody nieces, the little nobheads. So I crept into their room (they were all downstairs having breakfast) and I ransacked it, turfing everything out their wardrobes, looking for my stuff and not bothering to put anything back the way I found it. Why should I? I had no intention of ever coming back after today anyway. When I walked out that room you couldn't see the floorboards for clothes.

With my bag bulging like Santa's sack, I crept down stairs. I might as well have pogoed down though, because each wooden stair creaked like it was trying to snitch on me to Grandma, to Max's mother and the nieces. But the good thing about them being so bloody ignorant to me meant they never said good morning or goodbye as I left, so I could just walk out the front door and it wouldn't seem odd. I got to the bottom of the stairs. I put my hand on the front door. Took a deep breath.

'Rachel!' It was Max's mum. 'Come!'

My palms went instantly wet. I started shaking. I put the bag down in the hallway and walked as casually as I could – which was about as casually as I'd walk to the gallows – into the kitchen. They were all there, sitting around, cross-legged on the floor, chanting, 'Nam Myoho Renge Kyo, Nam Myoho Renge Kyo,' as they often did, being Buddhists. No men, they were all at work. But not just Max's grandma, mum, sister and nieces, but aunties and even neighbours.

'Sit!' I was ordered.

I did, my eyes flicking towards the hallway where my bag sat waiting to be found and my mind imagining the wailing that would tear through the house should one of these nieces pop upstairs at any point soon.

One of the neighbours had better English than any of Max's family, so she had been given the role of spokesperson, it seemed. 'The reason why your marriage is unhappy,' she began abruptly, 'is because you have not given your husband a baby.'

I wanted to punch the interfering old cow in the gob.

'If you give him a baby,' she said, 'you will make him happy. And if he is happy, you will be happy.' She smiled as if I needed a demonstration of what happy looked like. And at that stage in my life I think I probably did, but I was fuming again at the way these people were suggesting I was only there to serve a man's needs.

How bloody ironic, I thought, them all sitting around chanting a mantra which is central to a belief that happiness comes from within – they had clearly missed the entire point of it, not unlike millions of people in many other religions around the world. So I wiped my sweating hands on my trousers and took another deep breath to try and stop my voice shaking, then I said, 'Marriage is about love and equality. Or it should be anyway. No one is there to serve the other. It's not my job to make him happy. Now if you'll excuse me I have got a job to go to, *unlike you lazy tarts!*' OK, I didn't say that last bit, but I got up, all unsteady like some newborn lamb, and I marched out, taking my bag and not looking back.

I couch surfed for the next few weeks at Maggie's and Douglas's and then Moira's too, but I couldn't do it forever. They were all great, very supportive, but I knew I'd outstay my welcome soon enough. I needed to get my passport back and get home to England, but how was I going to do that without bumping into Max or one of his family or even the interfering neighbours? I was too scared to go to the house myself. God knows what Max would've done if he'd seen me. Perhaps he'd make good on one of his threats at last.

It turned out that that student Kyomi didn't think I was so mental after all. She and I used to get the same train home after school as she lived round the corner from Max's place. She had begun to ask questions on one of our train journeys home before I ran away. I found myself confiding in her and then, once I'd left, she told her parents about my situation and they, bless them, offered to put me up for a while too. They were just so good to me. A very traditional Japanese couple, so much so that when I turned up on their doorstep with my bags gratefully trying to hug them, they just kept bowing and I kept trying to hug, and I'd miss as they kept bowing, but somehow in the end I made it inside. I sat in their house that night sobbing my heart out, thinking how alien they must think me, like Max's family did, for complaining about my husband, but Yuki, Kyomi's mother, just leant forward and put her hand on mine. 'You do not have to prove anything to anyone by staying,' she said softly. 'It is OK to leave.'

After a few days, Tomoki, Kyomi's father, went round to Max's to ask for my passport. I didn't know he was going to do that and, even though I was grateful to him for trying, I was scared someone would have followed him back to the house and found out where I was.

'I'm sorry,' Tomoki said. 'I tried. I saw Max. He was there with his friend, a big man. Max said he did not have your passport. I thought they might get angry if I kept insisting he had it, so I had to leave.'

'It's OK,' I said. 'Thank you for trying.'

Max, you lying bastard, I thought.

And then there was a heavy fist pounding on the front door and my worst nightmare was realised. Jimmy, who must have been the big man Tomoki had seen at Max's, was standing outside looking more than a bit pissed off.

4

AN ENGLISH GENTLEMAN

'Shit, he followed Tomoki home,' I thought, as Jimmy continued to beat his massive fist on the door.

Kyomi, her parents and I all looked at each other, eyes like saucers, wondering what to do.

It was clear from the way Jimmy was knocking that he wasn't going anywhere until someone answered the door, but I was terrified if I was the one who opened it he would grab me and march off back to Max's with me tucked under his enormous arm as if I was nothing more than the morning paper.

Tomoki eventually did his duty, as the man of the house, and with a trembling hand opened the door. They exchanged a few words. I peered round the corner to try and work out just how angry Jimmy was. As he continued to talk to Tomoki, I realised he was more upset than angry, and when he saw me over Tomoki's shoulder he burst into tears and called out to me, apologising for Max. He cried and he cried like the big cuddly bear I knew him to be and before long we had him inside with a coffee.

'I cannot believe how Max is treating you,' he snivelled through the steam coming up from his cup. 'He is lucky to have you. He should never behave so badly. I am so sorry, Rachel. So sorry. Please do not think we are all like this.'

'I don't, you nobhead,' I said giving his shovel of a hand a little squeeze.

'I am here to help,' he said wiping his eyes. 'What can I do to make this better?'

'Well…' I said, treading carefully, 'I really need my passport back first. Max has stolen my passport from me. Can you get it back for me, Jimmy? Can you?'

I called my mate Sharon, who had been on tour with me the very first time I had ever met Max and Jimmy. I had kept in touch with my mates back home, but as I did with my mum, I'd started to call them all less and less because I was so ashamed of the way my life had gone and I couldn't tell them the truth. But now I saw some light at the end of the tunnel. I knew I could take some control back if Jimmy helped me, so I called Sharon and told her everything. She couldn't believe it. Couldn't believe sweet, gawky Max had turned into such a monster.

I called my mum too and broke down as soon as I heard her voice.

'I'm coming to get you,' she said firmly.

'No, no, you don't need to. I'm coming home.'

'But how?'

'I've been saving my money for a ticket since I left Max. And now,' I said smiling up at Jimmy who was standing in the middle of Kyomi's living room again. 'I've got my passport back, haven't I.'

Kyomi and her parents were running alongside the car crying and waving as Jimmy drove me to the airport. Even though I couldn't wait to get out of Japan, I was so sad to leave them. I would really miss them but I knew I would see them again one day; I would make sure of it. But I still told Jimmy to step on it, get out of there fast before Max came running round the corner after me. As I hurried through the airport, my heart was still going like the clappers and I don't think it slowed down until we were in the air and I was sure I was free.

When I got back to England, back to my mum in Bebington, I was a wreck. She sent me to the doctor's straight away and they prescribed antidepressants – Prozac to be precise.

Back then, in the late nineties, all I'd ever heard about Prozac was Americans getting hooked on it and committing suicide. So I told them where to shove it. I went to see various counsellors. Or rather, I was *sent* to see various counsellors. I was in such a state that I couldn't do anything for myself. I could barely walk without someone saying, 'You put one foot in front of the other.' I couldn't think for myself. I didn't want to be in this world anymore. I had thoughts about ending it all, but I couldn't do it. I couldn't do it to my mum. She'd already lost my dad. I couldn't put her through all that again. Besides, I probably wouldn't have had the guts to go through with it. I just wished that I could go to sleep and not wake up – not wake up as me, but wake up as my dad so I could give him back to Mum.

'Look Rachel,' she said as she saw me spiralling further and further down, 'if you had a broken arm you'd put it in plaster, if you had a headache you'd take a paracetamol. Now, if you need a tablet to mend your mind, why don't you take one?'

She had a point. And since that point was coming from Mum, who I knew wanted nothing but the best for me, I decided I'd give it a go.

The doctor told me it might take a couple of weeks for the Prozac to kick in, and he was right. I felt nothing until the very day I was due for a check-up with a mental health nurse. I went in there buzzing, flying high. And the nurse who was expecting to see a depressed patient was baffled. She started wondering if I was bipolar, which I wasn't, she'd just caught me coming up on the Prozac.

For so long my entire insides had felt like they were in complete darkness. Pitch black. With the medication I could feel myself climbing a ladder and it was getting brighter and brighter with every step but, no matter how much brighter it got, there was still this fist of darkness in my head that no amount of Prozac could ever get rid of. And that wasn't helped when Max turned up on my mum's doorstep.

When I saw him through the window I actually vomited, but for some reason I might never understand – curiosity? And we all know what that did, don't we – it didn't stop me then opening the door and inviting him in. He was with an interpreter. He was leaving nothing to chance. Nothing was going to get lost in translation this time. We sat in the back garden with my mum and he explained himself through this interpreter.

'I have come to England to show you that I can be a gentleman. A proper English gentleman.'

I saw my mum's eyebrows creep up her forehead in disbelief.

'I didn't want an English gentleman,' I told Max. 'I wanted you. At least the you that I knew in the beginning.'

'I can stay for three months. Can you give it a try for just three more months? I promise you, you will be happy with me again.'

I saw my mum's face screw up, unimpressed. It made me recall all my friends and family who had been cynical about Max in the first place. In fact they'd been downright prejudiced. When I'd told them I was marrying Max, they'd say things like,

42

'What you marrying a Jap for? If your dad was alive he'd shoot him. Do you know what the Japs did in the war?'

'What has the war got to do with Max?' I'd snap back. 'He wasn't even born then.'

All this racism rang round my head as we sat in the garden that day and it made me want to show them all how wrong they had been about Max, even though I was afraid they were right – at least about him not being right for me. And then I imagined all the Japanese gossips saying how I didn't try hard enough to make my marriage work – yep, I was still all over the place – and I thought, 'I've stuck out two and a half years, what's another few months? At least I can say I really did try then.'

'OK,' I said.

My mum nearly fell off her patio chair.

'But this time we do it in England.'

So we rented a house in Chester and Max was as good as gold... to begin with.

One day we went for lunch at a Japanese restaurant near the house. Japanese restaurants were not two a penny in England back then, like they are nowadays. The Japanese owner was there at the time and she started chatting to us, fascinated to hear Max was my husband. And even more fascinated to hear he wasn't a bad cook. And then she came out with, 'Do you want a job? We need someone to do all the prepping, the tempura, that kind of thing.'

Max jumped at the chance. And at the same time she offered me a job, as the manager. Everything was falling into place.

After work Max would often bring his fellow chefs – all Japanese too – back to the house, and they would have a drink. Or three. Around his Japanese mates it was like he was back in Japan again and he would order me about. But this time I would answer back.

'Hey, woman,' said one of the chefs, 'You must do what he say!'

Well, I, of course laid into this bloody bloke, while Max sat there doing nothing, but filling his face with beer.

And then as the weeks went on, the nastiness returned. The jibes and the criticisms. Then the threats. I could see it all happening again. Max, the English bloody gentleman, was a monster again. So after about a month, I got up in the middle of the night and just cycled the hour's ride back to my mum's in my pyjamas.

The next day he was on the doorstep with the same interpreter begging for forgiveness. He didn't need a bloody interpreter when he was making those threats and sniping at me, did he.

'No, no, no,' I cried. 'We're finished. Never again.'

He told me he was going to go to London for some reason, that he was going to get a job and prove to me he could be this gentleman he kept going on about.

'You do what you want,' I told him. 'We're done.'

I knew his address in London. I needed it to go ahead with the divorce proceedings. One of the other chefs in the restaurant – a nice one called Kohei – told me he went to visit Max there a couple of times. Once, he wasn't even in at the time they'd arranged to meet and the other time Kohei peered through the letterbox to see Max was comatose on the floor after a drinking binge.

I never saw Max again. In fact that whole three-year period soon began to feel like a horror movie I'd watched. Something so awful that it couldn't have really happened to me. If I think back to the depression I was in at that time, I never ever thought I would be OK again. I couldn't see how I could be happy. But it was such a bizarre episode in my life, so unreal, that in a way that helped me get over it. Despite that, the fist of darkness in my head remained and I still needed the antidepressants to keep my grip on that ladder to the light.

Now I was finally free of Max, I threw myself into work. Because I was running the Japanese restaurant, wearing all sorts of hats there, and because I saw that Japanese cuisine was up and coming in the north of England, I decided I'd open my own Japanese restaurant. You'd think I'd want to forget about anything connected with Max and Japan, and some psychologists might have a field day with my decision, but the owner of the restaurant had encouraged me to do it, and I may be crap at many things, but I knew I was good with people and PR. And when I get an idea in my head, I go for it, lock, stock and barrel, for better or worse.

I went to Southport, about forty-five minutes north of Bebington. It was full of Yuppies at the time. Famous footballers lived there. It was the perfect place to open a trendy restaurant. I got a hand from a mate writing a business plan and the bank lent me forty-five thousand pounds. I found a double-fronted shop just off the beaten track. It wasn't the nicest street in Southport, to say the least, but I was convinced that it didn't matter where we were, as long as the food was good, people would come. I found a chef from London, Japanese waitresses from a Japanese college, sourced their kimonos and spent the whole of the bank loan doing the place up. It had seventy seats when I'd finished with it and it looked beautiful. The first year trading it was chock-a-block. We even won restaurant of the year in *Lancashire Life* magazine and had visits from all sorts of celebrities – some of which I won't mention here because in recent times they've been locked up for various crimes. I will though mention superstar Liverpool footballer Jamie Redknapp and his dad Harry Redknapp who was managing West Ham United at the time.

But the second year went strangely quiet. And being a bit green when it came to running a business, I had spent all the loan on doing the place up, which left me nothing for a rainy day like this. I had to start working in Marks and Spencer in Southport and doing all the overtime they had going. I'd go in at half six in the morning till half five, then I'd rush to the restaurant and do all the prep so I didn't have to pay the chef for those two hours. I moved into a grotty bedsit to save money, where I had to share a mouldy bathroom with five other tenants. All the money I earned at Marks and Sparks I spent on my staff's wages. And I wasn't shrewd enough – or dodgy enough, depending on how you look at it – to realise that if I'd just not declared a grand of the takings we wouldn't have passed the threshold to be VAT registered. When the VAT bill came, it was humungous and I couldn't afford to pay it. Things started to go downhill. I had to let some staff go and, in the end, I decided to voluntarily shut up shop, before I was shut down for not being able to pay the bills.

Late in the day I was introduced to an accountant who would help me tie everything up and save me as much money as he could. He told me that I still owned all the fixtures and fittings and I could sell the lot and make some money back, but I would need to get it all out of the restaurant and put it into storage as soon as possible.

I did as he told me.

And the arsehole did a runner with it all.

*

I was plunged back into that darkness. And I was back with my mum.

Mum was my rock. The best thing in my world. I suppose you might call me the black sheep of the family. It was always me who cocked up. No one else in our family had been divorced. No one else had lost a business. But my mum never judged me, she was and is simply always there for me.

As I licked my wounds at Mum's house, I was feeling a bit thick after this most recent failure. I'd left school with no qualifications and so I enrolled in college to get the Access to Higher Education Diploma, a qualification that prepares students – usually mature students like me – for study as an undergraduate at university. Not that I was planning to go to university, but I just wanted to prove to myself that I could do it.

And I did.

But when that was all done with, I needed to just feel normal. Get a job and keep my head down like normal people do. And so I ended up working for Bank of America as a telemarketer. I didn't like it, but normal people don't like their jobs, do they? They go to work, earn their crust and come home and watch telly or something. They also have boyfriends, girlfriends, partners, husbands and wives. I wasn't desperate to get into another relationship, but back at my mum's I started meeting up with people I hadn't seen for ages, people I'd grown up with. People like Trevor.

Trevor's family moved to our road when I was seven and he was two. I used to push him around the close in his pram as his mum watched us from the window. When I got back from Southport I started to see him again. And we started going out. We'd known each other forever, so it was easy, we both knew it felt right. And we fell in love.

I was not in love with my job though, but I did like the organisation, and I worked hard enough that I was promoted to the role of underwriter and was then offered a job in America itself for three months teaching the UK way of assessing the creditworthiness or risk of a potential borrower by analysing their credit history, collateral and capacity. I know, I sound dead clever, don't I? I was put up in a nice big house in Delaware, given a car to get around in and Trevor even came out for a week. It was fab – a little taste of the good life.

Back in the Wirral, Trevor and I had been together about nine or ten months when I decided to stop smoking. It was 2004. I was thirty-five and I'd been a proper heavy smoker all my adult life, so I thought it was about time. It turned out it was easy. But then the girls at work started saying things.

'Ey, Rach, your boobs.'

'What about them?' I said looking down.

'They're getting bigger.'

'How do *you* know?' I squealed, pulling my blouse shut at the collar.

'You can't miss 'em.'

'I'm just putting a bit of weight on I s'pose. What with giving up smoking.'

A few days later it was, 'Ey, Rach, look at your nails!'

'What about them?'

'They've never been long.'

'I've stopped smoking, so of course they're going to grow. I'm healthier, arn' I.'

'You're not bloody healthier. The boobs, the nails, the weight. You're bloody pregnant.'

'I'm not bloody pregnant. I can't be pregnant.'

Don't get me wrong, I dreamed of being pregnant, but I knew I could never have a baby naturally because I had polycystic ovaries. That's why I couldn't give Max the child the interfering old bags in his family insisted would make him happy, and I'd never hidden the fact. Polycystic ovaries is a condition whereby you have infrequent, irregular or prolonged periods, and the ovaries develop small collections of fluid and fail to regularly release eggs. No eggs, no baby. I'd known it for years and I'd come to accept it.

''Ere you are. Go and do that!' one of the girls said to me, shoving a pregnancy test at me.

'Don't be daft,' I said, sticking it in my drawer. 'What did you waste ten quid on that for?'

I was really annoyed she'd done that, but as I got on with my work I was conscious of this thing in my drawer, as if it was calling to me. A couple of days later, when I'd finished all my tasks, I was bored enough to think, 'Right, I'll go and pee on that stick. Show them, like.'

So I sloped off to the toilet. Had a wee. Looked at the little screen.

You are pregnant.

I flew out of the toilet so fast, flashing the tester in everyone's face, grinning like a loony. I was bawling my eyes out when I bumped into my manager.

'Look at that! Look at that!' I said nearly poking his eye out with the tester.

'Calm down! Calm down!' he said studying the little screen. Then he looked up at me, 'Does Trevor know?'

I shook my head.

'Then get yourself off home and tell him the good news, love!'

I didn't need to be told twice. I raced home and told Trevor. We danced around the kitchen. It was the best day of my life. We raced over to my house and I presented my Mum ceremoniously with the pregnancy test thingy.

She turned it over in her hands for a moment then said, 'What's this?'

'Look at it, Mum!'

'I am, but what is it?'

Trevor and I were hopping about, bursting.

'Oh, for God's sake, Mum, we'll be here all day.' I pointed to the little screen for her. She put on her glasses and inspected it more closely.

After what seemed like half an hour she looked up. 'You can't be. You can't have kids.'

'Well, I can now,' I squealed.

As Mum tried to regain the power of speech, Trevor said, 'Let's go and tell my mum and dad!'

'What, now? At this time?'

'Yeah, I can't wait.'

'But they're in Lancaster visiting your uncle all weekend. It'll take two and a half hours just to get there.'

Trevor's face dropped and he grumbled, 'If your mum was away somewhere you'd have gone and told her in person, wouldn't you?'

I couldn't argue with that, so we got straight in the car and drove all the way up the M6.

'So you'll be getting married now,' said Vic, Trevor's dad, in a tone that was worryingly similar to the way Trevor grumbled before we left home that night.

Vic was dead old fashioned. The type who believed women should be seen and not heard. Traditional, let's say.

'Why would we get married?' I said. 'We've both been married before and we were both dead unhappy.'

Trevor had to nod in agreement.

'Besides we don't need a piece of paper to show how much we love each other.'

Vic looked at me as if I'd just farted really loudly.

A matter of weeks before Sam was born, I had a sudden panic: if we didn't get married then my child would not have the same surname as me, it would have Trevor's name. I didn't even know that our baby could take my surname, or both our surnames; that was far too New Age, far too Yuppyish for a working-class family from Bebington. I loved my surname because it was my dad's too, but if getting married meant my baby and I would have the same name then married we must be!

So, fit to pop, we hastily tied the knot. Just in time as it turned out, because four weeks later in April 2004 the contractions started.

Me, being me, had got another big idea in my head, that I would not have an epidural during the birth. But after thirty-one hours of painful labour, as I stood there gripping the side of the bed, mooing like a cow with her udders caught in the barn door, the midwife said to me, 'Rachel, you don't get extra Brownie points for not having medication, you know.'

I whimpered back, 'Will it make the pain go away?'

'Of course, love. Immediately.'

'Oh, bloody hell, give it here then!'

It was just as well, because things weren't quite right and soon after I was rushed to the operating theatre for a

C-section. But after many nail-biting minutes when my mum smoked just about all the fags she had left on her, our beautiful baby boy Samuel was born.

I'd never claimed any benefits in my life, but Trevor said we should ask about child benefits, now we had one. He offered to sort out all the paperwork, which was fine by me as I didn't know anything about it, but then his application was denied, because apparently he earned too much money – he ran his own business selling uniforms and workwear all over the world, from school uniforms to construction site gear.

Not getting the benefits didn't bother me at the time because I was made up with my new little family. Those night terrors I'd had when I was a little girl, worrying myself silly about dying before I'd done something amazing; perhaps it wasn't the dancing that was the amazing thing I was meant to do. I thought this was it: being a happily married stay-at-home mum was the thing, because it felt bloody amazing to me.

The only trouble was, as soon as Trevor became a father, he started to change.

5

GENUINE FAKE

We didn't hang about after Sam was born. We wanted another baby and we got on with trying. But this time it wasn't as easy and we soon had to admit defeat – at least doing it the natural way. So we tried Clomid, a tablet you can take as a fertility treatment, and ovarian drilling, which luckily didn't involve someone wielding a Black and Decker. It worked a treat. Benjamin was born in December 2006.

I was made up to be the proud mother of two beautiful healthy kids. I still couldn't believe it had happened. But I was not so happy with the way Trevor was turning out.

He was so controlling now. It started with the tiniest of things. Like, if I was cooking in the kitchen, he would waltz in and turn the gas down under the pot I was using until he was happy with it and then bugger off out again, as if he was Gordon bloody Ramsay. Then it was things like holidays; any holiday we had, the destination was chosen by him. Very soon it began to dawn on me that not just holidays, but everything was his way or no way. If he wanted something, we could afford it. If I or the kids wanted something, we couldn't.

I wasn't allowed to do the supermarket shop because I would always see extra bits in Tesco that I thought might be nice for the kids, so I'd chuck them in the trolley too. Trevor would stick religiously to the list we'd made before we left the house, so he soon made me stay at home. He said I was no good with money, that I was wasting it.

After getting married, I'd moved in with Trevor, in the house he had once shared with his brother. When I'd wanted to brighten the place up with a lick of paint, he'd stopped me. Even when Ben was born and it was time to paint his room, I had big ideas to make it magical. Trevor gave me a choice of two blues, one of which was pretty much the same colour as the old wallpaper that was already hanging there.

Trevor loved the finer things in life and he made sure he got them by putting all his effort into the business. But if I wanted to treat the kids to a trip to the cinema, he'd say, 'Take 'em to the park, it's free!'

And if we were at the bloody park and I wanted to buy them an ice cream from the café there he'd say, 'Go to Aldi and buy a box of 'em! Why should I pay these extortionate prices?'

Yet he would do things sometimes that would totally confuse me. For example, I was laid up on the couch with flu one day, when he took the boys out to the Cheshire Oaks shopping centre. When they got back, he had bought me five – not one, ladies and gentlemen, but five – Radley handbags. I mean, what the hell was I going to do with five handbags? I wasn't even a handbag kind of girl.

'But they're Radley, aren't they,' he goes, 'designer and all that.'

He thought I would be made up. That really spoke volumes. They must have cost a fortune, those bags.

'I'd much rather have had the money to take the kids somewhere nice,' I told him.

He ignored me and said, 'Look, it's genuine leather that.'

I would have much preferred a genuine hug.

6

HAPPY PILLS OR HAPPY PLACE?

I was in the kitchen washing the dishes, looking out the window over the garden which was covered in frost. The sun had barely bothered to rise all day and the trees were black skeletons against the pasty sky. Ben was still a newborn. Sam was up in his room playing with him. I could hear them laughing together. I heard the front door open and heavy boots clumping straight up the stairs. I stopped scrubbing the greasy pan in the bowl and every hair on the back of my neck shot up as I heard a scream.

Then silence.

As I gripped the edge of the sink, my eyes still glued to the wintery garden, the same heavy boots came down the stairs again. I clenched my jaw tight as I found the strength to turn around and see this bloke standing in the kitchen doorway with Sam and Ben's severed heads hanging by the hair from each of his fists.

Of course, Sam and Ben weren't really in at the time. There was no intruder in the house, no beheadings. I was hallucinating. Post-partum psychosis they call it – associated with postnatal depression. It was all part of my ongoing struggle with depression. I'd had prenatal depression too and I'd had the lot with all my kids including Harriet, my third, who was born in February 2011.

When she was still tiny, I decided I was going to take Harriet to the zoo. So we went to the one in Chester, and as we got to the big cats section, someone rushed over, grabbed her from the pushchair and drop kicked her over into the lions' cage where she was quickly torn apart. It was just another one of those hallucinations, but I could never watch *The Lion King* in the same way again.

What with the psychosis, Trevor's controlling behaviour and me putting on tons of weight after having three kids, I'd kissed goodbye to my dancer's body and with it my self-esteem. My body was my only asset when I was younger – it was what people complimented me on when I was on stage. I'd always been scared that, if I lost that, I'd have nothing.

'Run!' Trevor's mate Pete said.

I was just about to jump up from the kitchen table and scarper out the door, thinking he'd seen a real intruder this time, until I got what he was on about.

'Running is really good for getting the weight off.'

He'd popped round to see Trevor, but when I told him he wasn't in, Pete stayed for a cuppa anyway. He was a sweet bloke, a very peaceful soul. He'd just agreed to be Harriet's godfather and I was made up about that. He was planning on taking the role very seriously.

As we chatted over our hot drinks, I'd told him how frumpy I felt and how I was desperate to make a change, but I had no idea how to do it. I felt I was too deep in this rut to ever get out now. When he started talking about exercise, I remembered this poster I'd seen on the noticeboard outside the school gates.

'Well, they've got this Zumba class at the boys' school on Wednesday night,' I said.

'What's that? Sounds like a Disney movie.'

'No, you nobhead, it's like dance and fitness rolled into one.'

Pete turned his nose up. 'I think there's nothing better than running myself. Pound those streets, girl! Trust me, the weight will drop off.'

'I'll think about it,' I sighed. Then changed the subject. 'You all set for the christening tomorrow?'

'Yes,' Pete grinned. 'Can't wait. Me, a godfather. Who would have thought!'

I was looking forward to it so much too, but I was dead anxious about how Trevor was going to be. He had been all right (not wonderful, but all right) about Ben and Sam's christenings, and then when the vicar came round to talk to us about Harriet's, Trevor was a nightmare. He refused to respond to the vicar at first, but when the vicar directed more questions at Trevor, he stropped, 'I don't know why we're having her christened anyway.'

'Don't be so rude,' I said, wanting the earth to swallow me up.

'Well,' the vicar said, apparently unshaken, 'clearly it is important to Rachel, so will you get involved to support your wife and little Harriet?'

'Oh, well,' Trevor moaned, 'I'll come, like, but I don't believe in any of it. Look when you're dead you're dead and that's it. It's all a load of shite really.'

I was mortified. I apologised profusely to the vicar and told him, no matter what Trevor said or did, I wanted Harriet christened because I didn't believe it was a load of old... If I was honest, I wouldn't say I was a believer either, but I told the vicar the tradition meant a lot to me. All my family had been christened and I felt it was a beautiful way of welcoming someone to the world. The vicar was satisfied with that.

Harriet looked so gorgeous on the day in her christening dress. I took her proudly to the front pew where I was supposed to sit with the boys and Trevor. But after a few minutes I turned round to see where Trevor had got to. He was sitting on the pew behind me with Pete and the rest of his mates. When our eyes met, he smirked. Jenny, his mum, was furious. She kept hissing at him to move to the front with his family, but he shooed her away and folded his arms, that smirk still stuck to his gob.

The vicar directed his speeches to me and when it came to the time for us to take Harriet to the font, Pete, as godfather, proudly stepped up. Trevor slouched towards the font and I was burning to tell him to stay where he was. We sang a hymn. Trevor stood there, lips tightly shut. I felt he was humiliating me as publicly as possible.

That night as I cradled Harriet in my arms, I sang to her, but I was singing to myself just as much, trying to sing the pain away.

'I'm Santa Claus as everyone knows, a fat man with a beard,
I'm dressed in red, silly hat on my head, but no one thinks I'm weird.'

It wasn't even Christmas, so I had no idea why that song written by the lad in the Port Sunlight Players all those years ago came to me, but it often did. It was one way I could escape, immersing myself in the fantasy world of my kids after Trevor had made a point of embarrassing me in front of our friends, which he did so often some of our oldest mates stopped inviting us round.

I couldn't stop thinking about what Pete had said about running, but I fancied the Zumba more to be honest. As

Wednesday approached, I reckoned the school was about a mile and a half away, so I thought to myself, 'Why don't I run to the Zumba class?' Typical me – all or nothing.

But then I was wracked with self-consciousness about the way I looked. I imagined everyone I passed in the street as I ran would be saying, 'Ooh, look at her! She was a professional dancer once. Fit as a fiddle, she was, like. She's really let herself go, hasn't she?'

So I put on big, loose jogging pants and a top, pulled the hood up to try and disguise myself and when it was dark enough I set off.

Sweating like a pig, my lungs on fire, I stopped to take a break, bent over, holding onto my knees like Zola Budd after the 5000 metres. But when I straightened up and looked over my shoulder I hadn't even done 500 metres. I was only just at the end of our road.

'Fuck me, this is going to be harder than I thought.'

I must have stopped again three or four times before I got to the school. I'm surprised they even let me in the Zumba class when I eventually got there – I must have looked like death; a dripping wet, red-faced version of death.

One of the other women was handing me a bottle of water and saying, 'Do you want a drink?'

I looked round at all the other women who all looked like size zeroes from where I was standing. 'I want a burqa.'

But once I got into it, Zumba was right up my street. Of course, having been a dancer, I picked up the moves in no time and for the next year I went to the Zumba class as often as I could. With Pete's promise about the weight dropping off if I ran still ringing round my head, I jogged to every class. Each time it got a little bit easier. And then I realised I was enjoying the running part so much that I started running just for the hell of it. The sense of freedom I got from it was addictive. Out in the world. Out from under Trevor's thumb.

My mum was happy to have the kids for an hour here and there while I went for a run because she could see what it was doing for me. The weight was dropping off and my self-esteem was piling on in its place.

Trevor wasn't in the least bit supportive. In fact, when I came home from a run saying, 'I did a mile in thirteen minutes, can you believe that?'

He'd just say, 'I did a mile in eight minutes.'

'When?'

'Well…' he said. 'When I was at school.'

I was seething. Why did he have to pull the rug out from underneath everything I did? Why couldn't he just be happy for me? He was supposed to be my husband for God's sake, my partner, my cheerleader.

In the school playground one day, as we were all waiting to pick up our kids, I heard a couple of mums talking about the Liverpool Half Marathon. I couldn't believe the words that were coming out of my gob but I heard me say to them, 'Can I do that with you?'

A half marathon! Thirteen miles! I could barely get to the end of our street last year. But, you know me now, I got one of those ideas in my head again. I thought, 'Why can't I do it?' But then I thought that about the Japanese restaurant in Southport. I thought that about getting married to Max. I thought that about having a fairy tale family with Trevor. However, these mums didn't look at me like I was mental. They didn't see a beached whale that had no hope of getting back to the ocean, because I wasn't, not anymore.

'You look fab,' said one of the girls from that first Zumba class that I hadn't seen in ages. 'I'm going to complain. It hasn't bloody worked for me.'

The mums – Bev and Ally – said yes and we started training together. I hardly knew them to begin with. Ally was a small, dark little bundle of motherliness, while Bev was a tall blonde Earthy soul. Bohemian Bev I would call her, but not like Mrs Burns who was trying so hard to be a hippy. No, Bev was as natural as the organic food she ate. And three months later, when we all tumbled across the finish line of the Liverpool Half Marathon together, we knew everything about each other. It's amazing what you find out about people when you run with them. And now we were sisters, united by our achievement.

Bev and Ally's husbands and kids were at the finish line, screaming and clapping and holding up their hand-painted banners: *Go Mummy!*

Trevor was there too. He'd reluctantly agreed to bring the kids along when I told him Bev and Ally's would be there. Except Trevor just stood there as we came over the line, Ben and Sam either side of him and Harriet in the pram, his face like thunder, Sam and Ben looking glum.

'Come on, come on,' he barked at me as I tried to celebrate with Bev and Ally and their families. 'Let's go now. These kids are a pain in the arse.'

'What's the matter?' I asked.

'Going on about bloody hot dogs all the time,' he said headbutting the air in the direction of the food stands all around the finish line.

'Well, it's a special occasion,' I said. 'It won't hurt to have one, will it?'

Trevor thought for a moment as if he was trying to work out what was so special about this occasion, then he said,

'No, no, we've got hot dogs in the cupboard at home. We can have them there.'

I was so embarrassed that I had to slope off while the others enjoyed the day, but in bed that night it was not so much the embarrassment that was keeping me awake – after all, these days, Trevor was making sure that was pretty normal for me in front of my friends. No, I couldn't sleep because I was pondering on what Bev had said as we stood panting at the finish line.

'I couldn't run another metre.'

'Nor me,' said Ally.

I wanted to agree with them, be in solidarity with them as I had been for this whole journey, but I couldn't. I just kept thinking of the time I couldn't run a mile to the Zumba class. Then how we ran five miles, then ten. Now we'd run thirteen. I thought, 'So why can't we run fourteen? Then fifteen. And so on.' Another one of my big ideas was taking hold.

'I'm doing it,' I said to myself. 'I'm doing the bloody London Marathon, arn' I.'

Trouble is, you can't just rock up and do the London Marathon. There's only a certain number of places available. One way to get a place is in the ballot system, but half a million people enter that from which only about seventeen thousand are chosen – I'd have more luck winning the lotto. The other major way in is to run for a charity which has bought places in the race – then you have to raise money for that charity by gathering sponsorship, and some charities have a minimum you must raise in order to race. About fifteen thousand people get in that way every year. The rest of the forty thousand who run each year have probably got places because they qualified with fast times. But I was no Zola Budd last year and I certainly wasn't this year, so I had no idea how I was going to achieve my latest bright idea.

Until Claire House Children's Hospice approached us.

Ally, Bev and I had raised a bit of money for them when we'd run the Liverpool Half, and now they asked us if we wanted to do the London. The other girls were still sure they couldn't run another metre, but I nearly bit the arm off the events manager when he dangled the possibility of a place in front of me. I set about hassling everyone I knew to sponsor me and started training harder than ever. I had to ask my mum to look after the kids a bit more.

'Sometimes I'll have to be out running for four hours though.'

'I don't mind, love,' my mum smiled. 'More time to spend with my grandkids. And besides, I can see it's doing you the world of good.'

I wouldn't dream of asking Trevor to look after the kids. So I did most of my training when they were at school and Trevor was at work. I would leave Harriet with my mum and when I came back knackered from a run, I still made sure Trevor's dinner was on the table before he got home and that all the housework was done.

'You should be home looking after the kids and the house not gallivanting round the streets. Who do you think you are? Mo Farah?' he would say.

Comments like that made my blood boil. How dare he tell me what *my* duties were! When I came out of hospital after Sam was born he went off skiing in Banff. He did ask me first actually, and when I said it would be fine some of my mates said, 'Bloomin' 'eck, you're good letting him swan off all that way, and so soon after you having the baby.'

'All that way? He's only going over the Channel.'

'You what?'

'To France.'

'Banff isn't in France, love,' they told me.

'Where is it then?'

'It's in bloody Canada.'

As time went on, I didn't mind him going off on all these holidays he went on with his mates because I liked the sense of peace in the house when he wasn't there. Me and the kids could take a break from treading on eggshells around him.

When he was around, if I ever got upset at the comments and the sniping, or the fact that we couldn't afford to do anything as a family but he could afford to go skiing, he'd just say, 'Oh, go and have one of your happy pills.'

But running was my medicine now. I was getting more and more depressed with Trevor, and yet when I was out running all that seemed to melt away. It was like meditation, but better for me because there was no way I could ever sit still long enough to actually meditate. However, from what I'd heard about meditation, that's what I was doing when I was running. It really sorted my head out. I might have been tensing all sorts of muscles, some I didn't even know I had, but as I ran the tension in my mind ebbed away with every stride and soon I didn't have a care in the world. I never worried about running fast either because that would mean I couldn't enjoy looking around me as I ran. I loved taking in the scenery. The Wirral has some beautiful areas many of which I didn't know were there until I started exploring them in this way.

With every mile I added to my training I was elated. The day I reached seventeen miles I couldn't wait to get home and tell my mum that I'd done it. I didn't bother telling Trevor of course. But with every mile I felt stronger and stronger. With every mile I felt more able to take on the world. I remembered how in awe I used to be of people that had done things like the marathon and then here I was doing twenty-two miles in my training sessions – apparently, that's as far as you needed to go in training – adrenaline would carry you over the last four miles, so they said.

I still wasn't the most experienced runner though and this sometimes showed in some of the choices I made. I went out on a twenty-miler one morning. The sun was shining, the sky was blue. I slipped on my leggings and vest-top, stuck my headphones in and off I went. I never really planned my routes, I just headed out towards the countryside. So there I was, going down these country lanes, no pavements, a couple of hours later, and those blue skies were getting darker and darker until the heavens opened. It was torrential, this rain. Day became like night and muggins here was in black leggings and black vest, so all the cars that passed were beeping at me after narrowly avoiding me as I suddenly appeared in their headlights out of nowhere. The two-way traffic was having to slow down for me. There was much shaking of heads from drivers and no doubt a load of swearing inside their lovely dry, warm cars. I wanted to tell them all how sunny it was when I set off, but I'm not sure they would have given a shit anyway.

The next car to drive past stopped beside me. A door flew open and a voice said, 'Get in!'

It was a police car. Two policewomen inside. 'Shit,' I thought. I did as I was told.

'I'M SO SORRY, SO SORRY, I'M GOING TO GET YOUR SEATS ALL WET, ARN' I!'

'Take your headphones off!' the policewoman who wasn't driving said.

I'd hardly realised I still had my music blaring and I was shouting everything I wanted to say to them. So I apologised for shouting at them, apologised constantly for everything, but they just laughed and asked me where was home.

I didn't have to think about it. I gave them my mum's address. She nearly had a coronary when she saw a police car pull up outside, but it didn't occur to me to go to *my* house – Trevor's house. My mum's was always the place that I felt *at home* and happy. The place where I'd grown up. The place where I got encouragement, not criticism; where I got arms around me, not the cold shoulder. I started to go there more and more whenever I had a few hours spare, not just when I needed to drop off Harriet while I trained. But of course, since Trevor's parents still lived opposite my mum, it would get reported back to Trevor that our car had been parked outside my mum's for a few hours in the daytime when I should have been back at the house doing the ironing or something, according to Trevor.

And then I started to worry that he had a point. Was I neglecting my duties as a housewife and a mother? The house wasn't as tidy as I liked it to be, but that was because I was too depressed to take pride in it these days. I'd much rather be out running – my happy place. But I knew for sure my kids never wanted for my love and attention.

As the London Marathon got closer I wasn't even nervous about it. I was just dead excited. I knew it wasn't a *race* for the likes of me. When I first started running I thought I was crap if I wasn't doing ten-minute miles, if I wasn't beating the times other people bragged about on social media. But I soon realised the competition was not against other runners, but against the voice in my head that kept hissing at me to give up and stop wasting my time. And this voice always sounded just like Trevor. So London was not a race for me, but an experience – an iconic one that people travel from all over the world to be part of – that I was going to enjoy every minute of.

'I'm off then,' I said on the Friday night I was due to go to London.

Trevor was watching the telly. He didn't even lift his head to say goodbye let alone good luck.

I would have felt so lonely going to London on my own that night without Bev and Ally to run with, but my mum and my Auntie Liney came along instead for support. Liney's real name is Irene, by the way, but our Lynne could never pronounce Irene when she was little, she said Liney instead and the name stuck.

We stayed at a Travelodge in Bromley for the weekend and met up with a friend who lived there and was dead into the whole thing. He took my mum and Liney under his wing and even did a PowerPoint presentation the night before to show us exactly where I was going to see Mum and Liney and at what mile as he ushered them round London on the Tube to various points so that in the end I would see them six times throughout the route.

Greenwich Park was crammed with thousands and thousands of people at the start – it was like being at Glastonbury Festival or something, but even better, because every single one of us had a common goal – it was electric.

And then we were off. I don't think I stopped grinning the whole way round. I high-fived every kid's hand on the side of the road, couldn't stop thanking everyone for their support, felt like I was famous as everyone called out my name – 'Go on, Rachel!' I wondered how they knew my name at first until I remembered it was printed on my runner's bib, but it didn't make me feel any less of a rock star, and when Big Ben finally came in sight, I got goose pimples. I didn't stop running once and when I came down Pall Mall I knew the end was in sight...

...and I was actually gutted. Gutted it would all be over soon. As I neared the finish line I noticed a guy who was running for the charity Help for Heroes. He was really struggling, he looked like he wouldn't make it, but we were so close so I shouted at him, 'Come on, come on! You can do it! If I can do it, you can.' That seemed to put a rocket up his arse and he started running again. We finished together and I stood there sobbing and sobbing with joy. I did it in four hours and seventeen minutes, but the time really was irrelevant to me. I had done it and that's all I needed to know.

7

EPIPHANY

I was back to running on my own in the Wirral. Just little old me and my thoughts and Elbow playing in my headphones. No Bev and Ally, no forty thousand fellow marathon runners, no crowds cheering us on. But I was on top of the world.

'I did the London Marathon. I've only gone and done the London Marathon, haven't I. I'm a mother of three and I bloody well did it. What do you reckon, Dad? Who would have thought it, ey? Are you proud of me?'

I still chatted to my dad on occasions. I had done everything for my dad since he died. When I opened the restaurant it was dedicated to him. Everything was dedicated to him, to make him proud, until it slowly started to sink in that he was never coming back, so it was a bit stupid doing stuff just for him. I think this realisation came about as I ran more and more. The more running I did, the more meditation time it gave me. But that didn't mean I couldn't chat to my dad now and then – keep him up to date on things I'd been doing *for me*.

As I continued to chat to him on this run, I suddenly had an overwhelming feeling. My entire body filled with a freezing sensation, but not a bad one. It was a rush. The runner's rush, they call it. And I found myself sobbing again thinking, 'Where the hell did that come from?' As I stood there at the side of the road I looked around me and inside of me and I could honestly say I had never felt so completely content – not since I was a child, when you don't have a care in the world, when nothing has yet come along to puncture your innocence. After my dad died I constantly wished I was a child again; wished for a life before loss, before grief. Now, dripping with tears and sweat in my running gear, I had never felt such peace, and although it only lasted for a moment, I could recall it for the rest of my life.

When I got home I didn't say anything to Trevor, of course, but I wanted to shout it from the rooftops, this feeling I'd just had. The modern-day equivalent of shouting from the rooftops is, of course, posting something on Facebook. So I logged on to Facey and wrote about this feeling I'd had and how I'd gone from an overweight wreck to something resembling human again. How I'd been prescribed Prozac, but I'd found better results complementing it with this drug called running. I poured my heart out, I didn't hold back, I told it all, just as I've told it in this book so far (in fewer words obviously), but I was dead honest. I posted it, made the post public and got into bed next to my husband who snored away, oblivious of these monumental moments that were changing my life.

When I'd returned jubilant from the London Marathon he was right where I'd left him, in his armchair, and he ignored me again. Can you believe it? I'd just achieved something great, if I do say so myself, I'd made a dream come true and he didn't even say well done.

My mum and sister were always there for me, I never doubted their love and support, but when you don't feel that from the person you've chosen to spend the rest of your life with intimately, you can feel, as I did, desperately lonely and isolated. That left me craving love and craving something I couldn't put my finger on at the time. Now I know it was a sense of community I was craving. But I didn't want to worry my mum or our Lynne – they had their own problems to deal with. Instead, these images of the local church I went to when I was a kid kept coming back to me. Now, I'm no Bible basher, I can tell you, but I remembered this cosy warmth that I used to feel whenever I sat in St Andrews Church in Bebington back in the day. It's a beautiful building set in a green churchyard full of trees – picture postcard stuff. It was there I went to Sunday school and to Brownies when I was little. There that I went to Girl Guides – until I got thrown out for kicking this bitch Jenny in the fanny, but she was taking the piss out of my stammer, so serves her right.

So I told Trevor that I felt like popping into St Andrews one Sunday.

'You what?' He laughed at me. Laughed like Jenny laughed at my stammer back in Guides. Perhaps I should have kicked him in the balls liked I kicked Jenny in the fanny, but I was too busy reeling from the knife his laughter had stabbed into my heart. He was supposed to be my rock. 'Well, if you're going you can bloody well take the kids with you. I'm not babysitting your kids while you go poncing about in a church. You don't even believe in God.'

He had no idea what I believed in. He'd never asked.

I went anyway, but I had Sam and Ben hanging off me and Harriet in a pram as I trudged up the stone path and then struggled down the couple of steps into the church itself. As

I fought to get the pram over the threshold it seemed like the whole congregation came to help me. An elderly gent came and took the pram for me and when I was stood there at the back, looking around at that special light that only stained glass can give a room, at the gorgeous wood and stone work that seemed to glow in that light, I was overcome by a cold, tingling sensation that washed through me, through every part of me, and I burst out crying. It was exactly the same feeling that I'd had when I was out running and talking to my dad in my head. A runner's rush I'd called it then, but I wasn't running this time, was I? At least, I wasn't jogging down some country lane in the Wirral, but I might have been running from something… or to something.

'Are you OK, dear?' a little old lady with a lovely cloud of white hair on her head said, putting a hand gently on my arm.

'Oh I am, yes,' I said. 'I just feel overwhelmed, that's all.'

'Come and sit down. Come on.' I let her lead me. 'I'm Sylvia.'

'Nice to meet you. Rachel… I'm Rachel.'

I went and sat next to her on a pew, while the boys went and joined in with a little service that the vicar gives for the first half hour for the youngsters. Then they're all taken over the road to the church hall – where I'd gone to Brownies and (for a short time) Guides – for the Sunday school. Harriet had been whining so Sylvia took her for a bit and she was soon fast asleep in her arms. I hadn't felt such a sense of belonging for ages. It was a real family. Not like the one I had at home with Trevor. For the entire service tears ran down my cheeks and I wasn't sure if they were tears of sadness or joy. I think they were both. Tears for what I didn't have at home, and tears for what I'd found here in this little church.

I went every week from then on. Sylvia was always keen to have a cuddle with Harriet. But after a couple of months she disappeared.

'Where's Sylvia?' I asked another friend I'd made in the congregation.

'Oh, didn't you hear, love? She passed away last week.'

I was devastated. It brought up the kind of feelings I'd had when my dad died. I couldn't stand the idea of not seeing Sylvia ever again, just as it totally bent my head when I thought that I might never see my dad again.

The church ran this coffee morning on a Friday where they also studied the Bible. Apart from getting me out the house and giving me an excuse to hang around more with my new friends, I thought I might find some answers in the Bible; answers about death. The tea and cake didn't go amiss either.

When Trevor heard I was going to Bible study he thought I was 'going loopy', but I'd much rather spend time with them than I would with him these days. Besides, as we picked apart verses from the Bible and I began to understand the symbolism a bit more, it all started to make a lot more sense. Gone were the days when I was Brownie age and I would sit in St Andrews watching the vicar's lips move without understanding a word he was saying. At the coffee mornings I would ask questions with a childish simplicity, which everyone seemed to appreciate. I wanted to believe what we read so much – because I wanted to believe I would see my dad again one day – but when Jesus healed a blind man or turned water into wine I would say, 'I'm so sorry, but you've lost me there. How can this be true?'

'Well,' one of the group would say, 'we don't know that it is true. But we don't know that it isn't true either.'

'So?'

'So we have to have faith. And faith can move mountains.'

I thought about the way I approached running. The way I'd simply believed I could do the London Marathon after the Liverpool Half. The way Bev and Ally thought anything more than a half was impossible for them. But I had faith then. Faith that I could do the impossible. And with that faith I did it.

8

TOGETHER ALONE

I logged into Facey one night when I'd got the kids off to sleep. I scrolled through endless reams of crap, cats dressed up like pirates, pictures of someone's dinner, videos of epic fails, conspiracy theories and fearmongering. And then I noticed the little red circle on the notification bell. It had a large number in it. I clicked on it. Apparently I had more than seventy comments on that post I'd made and hundreds more likes. I started to read the comments. They were all from women, women like me. They were telling me how they too had lost their confidence, if they'd had any to begin with; how they'd piled on the pounds, especially after childbirth; how they'd been fighting depression and low self-esteem for years and nothing seemed to help. Some of the women were friends of mine, some were local. Others were just mums at the school gates, who had seen me running all over the place. They said they'd seen a transformation in me and they wanted *whatever I was on*. Some said they read my post with tears in their eyes and they begged me for help in private messages which were building up in my inbox – I'd never been so popular. Some women I'd never heard of, but since

I'd made the post public it seemed to have reached people far and wide and it suddenly dawned on me that while I'd spent all those years feeling alone and hopeless and ugly, there were many, many women out there feeling the same thing.

But how did we feel so alone, if there were so many of us?

As I sat there scrolling through all these comments, I knew we had to band together somehow – then perhaps we wouldn't feel so alone anymore. But we couldn't do that sat on Facey, on the outer reaches of the internet. We had to get together in the flesh.

I wish I could do what you do, commented one woman.

You can! If I can do it anyone can, I replied, recalling what I'd said to get that bloke over the line who was running for Help for Heroes in the London Marathon.

But I couldn't do it on my own.

Then come and do it with me.

Really?

Meet me at the school gates at 7pm on Wednesday night and I promise you'll love it. All welcome!

Wednesday night came and I was stood at the school gates on my tod.

7:01 p.m. 'She's coming. I know she'll come.'

7:03 p.m. 'Bloody hell, where is she?'

7:05 p.m. 'Please come, please come. Please don't give up before you even start. Please, please, please. I know you can do this.'

7:06 p.m. 'Oh fuck it…'

'I'm not late am I?' It was her – the mum who I'd offered to run with.

'No. No, you're right on time,' I said, giggling with relief. 'I'm Rachel.'

'Keely,' she said, 'but everybody calls me Keels.'

'Nice to meet you, Keels.'

And then there were two more. And another. And before I knew it there were ten, all looking at me expectantly, all come to get a bit of *whatever I was on.*

'Oh my God,' I thought, suddenly feeling the weight of the responsibility. But I knew how to get rid of weight, didn't I. Run! 'And you better make sure they love every minute of it too,' I told myself. I suddenly felt like a teacher. I knew all too well from my time at school the power of a good teacher and I knew the power of a bad one. I wanted to be Mrs Reed to these girls, not Mrs Burns, so with a smile I turned to face the class.

'Room for one more?' It was my sister Lynne.

9

LYNNE

When I was thirty-nine, my husband Lew and I had been trying for a baby for a long time, but with no luck. It seemed I just couldn't get pregnant naturally and so Lew and I decided to start IVF. After three rounds of that I still wasn't pregnant. Everything had gone so well in the early stages, but each time the embryos had been implanted into my womb they just wouldn't embed. I was so frustrated. The doctors couldn't explain exactly why but back then in 2006 the IVF success rate was only 27 per cent. Had I done it these days I would have had a much better chance with a 65 per cent success rate. But I'm fifty-three now so it wasn't to be.

As each year passed, I could see that time was running out for us and it really started to get me down. When I was forty-six, I became really low, hitting rock bottom in fact. I was so depressed, feeling inadequate as a woman, a failure – typical feelings for someone in my position who wanted children so badly.

In a way, I took solace in my sister Rachel. She had been through the mill with her awful experience in Japan, and we both knew that wasn't helped by losing our dad when we were younger. We were very different growing up, so if anything good came out of Dad's death, it was that it brought us closer together. Just the sheer fact that she was at home more after being away dancing so often was a great comfort to me. We both dealt with Dad's death in different ways, but we could at least be together while we dealt with it. She had her problems getting pregnant too, so we could support each other, being in the same boat in more ways than one.

When the news came that she was pregnant in 2004 with Sam, I was over the moon for Rachel. And in 2006 when Ben came along too I was even happier. Of course I was sad for myself not having children, but I would never begrudge Rachel her joy. She had gone through so much trauma in her life already. I was so excited for my little sister. Ben was another miracle. Perhaps there was still hope for me too then.

But we soon had to call it a day with the IVF. Both Lew and I were gutted. That's when Rachel came to see me and said, 'You still have an embryo left from the IVF, don't you, love? Lew's bits are all fine, so perhaps you just need a different incubator for your baby. We know my incubator's working these days, so why don't I just carry your baby for you?'

'You mean like a surrogate?'

Rachel nodded. She was beaming at the idea. She so wanted to see me with a baby of my own. For a moment I felt my heart begin to race with the possibility, but then a thought occurred to me.

'What about if you need a C-section again?' I said.

'I checked with the doctor,' Rachel danced about, excited that she'd covered all bases already, 'and he said I could have one more C-section if I had to.'

'But you always wanted to have three kids. I know you're dying to have a little girl.'

Rachel hesitated. She tried to shrug it off. 'Yeah, but there's no guarantee I'd have a girl, is there?'

But I couldn't take that possibility away from her. 'No way, sis.' I hugged her. 'It's such a wonderful thing for you to offer. Thank you. But I want you and Trevor to have that third baby. Have that girl!'

It must have been a few months later when Rachel called me.

'Will you come round tonight with Lew? I want to speak to you both about something.'

Well, of course, I panicked. 'What's wrong? What's wrong?' I thought she had some terrible news to tell us.

'Nothing, nothing,' she reassured me. 'I just want to speak to you when you're here, that's all.'

Then the penny dropped and I burst out crying. 'Are you pregnant?' I sobbed down the phone.

After a pause she said, 'Yeah. I'm sorry, love, I...'

'No, no, don't you dare apologise! I'm so happy,' I told her, smiling through my tears. 'Have as many as you can and we'll share them, OK?'

'OK. OK,' she whispered.

When Rachel went into labour, Trevor offered to let me go and be with her during the birth instead of him. I suppose he must have been feeling sorry for me, since I wasn't able to have my own children and I'd passed up the opportunity of surrogacy so he and Rachel could have another. He came all the way to my workplace and picked me up in the car, took me to the hospital and then went straight home. I was a little surprised he went so quickly, but my overwhelming feeling was excitement at being by my sister's side for this moment.

Unfortunately the labour didn't go to plan and she had to have a C-section for the third time in her life.

'I want my sister! I want my sister!' Rachel shouted as she was wheeled into the operating theatre.

I hurried in and held her hand. She gripped mine for dear life.

'I can feel them cutting in to me,' she cried as the surgeon made the first incision.

'Are you sure, Rach? You've had the anaesthetic,' I said, although I was a bit concerned at the way it had taken a trainee three attempts to get the anaesthetic into Rachel's spine.

'Don't mistake pressure for pain,' said the surgeon as he cut again.

Rachel began to panic more now, convinced she was feeling the sting of a scalpel, so they gave her a general anaesthetic and sent me out of the room.

I nearly chewed my finger nails off as I waited. The operation seemed to go on forever. But then, at last, the midwife appeared carrying a little angel.

'Rachel says you have to be the first to hold her,' the midwife smiled, handing over the precious bundle. 'And we've been given strict instructions to take a photo of you kissing her forehead.'

We did just that and I burst into tears at the beauty of the moment; a moment I'll be forever grateful to Rachel for.

'And,' the midwife added, 'I hear they've called her Harriet *Lynne*.'

'Yes,' I beamed.

*

It was a couple of years later in the summer of 2013 when Rachel started the running club. I'd never run in my life, except at school on sports day, but when Rachel called me up talking so enthusiastically about the benefits, I thought I should consider it. Lew and I were still grieving for the children we could never have and we needed a distraction from that, a different goal, a focus. Lew had filled the void with golf, so he was more than happy for me to have a sport to take my mind off things too. Rachel was convinced it was just what I needed, but I was sure I wouldn't be doing any marathons like she did.

Nevertheless, I went along to her first session, to support her as much as anything. I turned up that first day in an old pair of leggings and a white T-shirt of Lew's that was so enormous on me it almost reached my knees. I was so self-conscious about my figure at the time, convinced everyone else was looking at me, when in fact, as I learnt later, everyone else was just feeling the same way.

'All you've got to do is run to that lamppost,' Rachel told us, pointing up the road.

Well, that wasn't too hard. Even I could do that. That lamppost was only fifty yards away, I reckoned.

But when we got to that lamppost, she told us to run to the next. Again that wasn't too far, so all ten of us just about managed that. And before we knew it, by running lamppost to lamppost, we were covering longer and longer distances. By the end of the second week, running twice a week, we were up to running a couple of miles in one go. We couldn't believe it. I hadn't felt so good in years, not because I was losing weight, but more because I'd achieved two miles. My confidence grew, which was helped by the fact that I could soon discard the big man's T-shirt and get into some new fitted running gear.

Rachel had taught us a breathing exercise: two breaths in through the nose then one out through the mouth. She had us running round the streets of Bebington doing this, but making noises with every breath to help us get into the rhythm. We got some funny looks from people passing by as we grunted and groaned, but that just sent us into fits of giggles, which Rachel encouraged. For someone who, by her own admission, had never been that interested in school, Rachel was a natural teacher. She taught us the things she had picked up when she was training for the marathon and as more and more runners came she sent herself off to a leadership course held by the England Athletics Association. She was keen to make sure she had some qualifications to back up her experience and make sure she wasn't doing more harm than good. But I had no doubt from the start she was doing us nothing but good. I was so proud of her.

She could be firm if we needed it, like a boot camp drill sergeant, but she was funny with it. We laughed a lot and that kept us going. Even when we might be dying to stop, she'd shout, 'LEG IT!' and we did, grinning all the way. She had us doing some exercises in pairs and, when we had enough breath to, when we weren't groaning and grunting, we'd start chatting, opening up. Before long you'd realise how everyone had their different reasons for being there and it was never just about losing weight. It quickly became more than a running club. It was a social club and a support group. A sisterhood.

10

HIGH VIZ

I called it Mums to Marathons, simply because I was a mum and I'd done a marathon, but it didn't mean you had to be a mum or had to do a marathon to join. Any woman could come along at whatever level and, as word got out, they did. In their droves. After only three months we had between fifty and sixty women running every week in the little town of Bebington alone. All shapes and sizes and all ages. I managed to get all of them ready for a local 10K run, but trying to train fifty-odd girls with different needs and abilities was too much in one group, so I had a word with our Lynne and another one of the girls, Clare, who was fast becoming one of my besties since she'd started running with us. They had both taken to running like a couple of Kelly Holmeses, so I asked them if they would go on the same runners' leadership course that I had done when the group first began to swell. Luckily for me, they jumped at it.

Then I started getting messages on Facey from women in other towns who wished they had a club like Mums to Marathons in their area. What could I do? I couldn't let them miss out on this secret I'd discovered, this wonder drug that no pharmaceutical company could ever manufacture. Since I'd been running, I had given up all the shrinks and mental health appointments which I had been going to ever since I escaped from Japan. I just didn't need them anymore. Running was my remedy and this gathering of girls was my new support system. I hoped that I was saving our wonderful NHS thousands of pounds a year by not going to the psychologists and mental health nurses anymore. And I wasn't the only one. Like our Lynne, so many of the runners found a new focus, a new boost to their self-esteem and a revitalised social life just by turning up twice a week and running up and down the streets of the Wirral, rain or shine. But now that I was a bit more experienced I wouldn't let any of us go out without the proper gear, reflectors and lights so we were safe and we could be seen in the dark and wet evenings. I didn't need the police picking me up like they did that rainy day last year. I don't think they'd be as sympathetic now there were fifty of us if we were stopping traffic and risking lives. No, now we looked like the Coca-Cola train at Christmas as we snaked through the country lanes with all manner of flashing lights and high viz stuff hanging off us.

So I found myself going round setting up clubs and leading sessions in Wallasey, Morton and Prenton too. It meant I was running a stupid amount of miles a week, but I couldn't let the girls down, could I. That amazing thing I always felt I needed to do since I was a little girl; the thing that kept me up at night worrying I'd snuff it before I had a chance to do it; this was it, I was sure now. But that meant I found myself in a new race – the race to share my epiphany with as many women as I could before my number was up.

I stopped going to church and the Bible study groups around this time, partly because we often ran on a Sunday morning since it was convenient for many of the women with their busy lives as wives and mothers and full-time employees, but also because I had found a new church, a new religion and there was nothing about this one I didn't believe in.

'You should start charging us all for this,' said Clare as she tried to catch her breath one night between runs.

'Yeah,' said our Lynne, 'I'd pay.'

'Oh, no,' I said, 'I can't charge people to run on their own streets.'

'Yeah, but it's not just running on the streets, you know what I mean, like,' Clare said with a tut. 'You've coached us. I wouldn't be able to get to the end of our bloody road otherwise.'

Lynne added, 'People pay a fortune to be shouted at in those boot camps in the park. And we'd all much rather be here having a laugh with you.'

With her words ringing around my head, I went home and googled those boot camps and saw they were charging about five pounds a session. I couldn't charge that much, but I suggested three quid a session or a fiver for two in one week.

The girls virtually chucked their fivers at me.

Jane was in her thirties and overweight when she joined Mums to Marathons, but she managed to get fit enough to do the Wirral Half Marathon. As we ran the course Jane spotted her sister up ahead – her slimmer, fitter, more glamorous sister.

'I'd love to cross the finish line before her... one day,' she huffed.

'One day?' I thought to myself. 'Why not today?'

Jane had opened her heart to me as we'd trained, just like all the other girls did to me and each other – it was our own brand of therapy – and I'd realised that Jane had always felt second best to her sister in everything: in her job, in her social life, in her love life, in her looks, in the family dynamic. So wouldn't it do her the world of good to come first for once? And here was the perfect opportunity.

But Jane was flagging. She needed an energy boost. So I reached in my bumbag that was always stuffed with energy bars, gels and all manner of goodies to keep me going.

'Have a jelly baby!' I said, handing her a red one.

'Have a jelly baby?' Jane panted. 'I feel like a jelly baby right now, my legs are wobbling all over the place.'

She chomped it down. And another. And with a bit of encouragement from me we came up alongside Jane's sister. I could see she was struggling as much as Jane was so I offered her something from my bottomless bumbag too. And then I winked at Jane and whispered, 'Come on, let's go.'

This time I had to pull out my best motivational cries from my internal bumbag, screaming at Jane to find the reserves of energy and willpower I knew she had somewhere. As we crossed the finish line, I never mentioned that she'd beat her sister. Mums to Marathons was never about racing. 'It's the finish line, not the finish time,' was the mantra I used to tell them all, which I'd coined when I was soaking up the scenery as I trained for my first marathon, but in this instance I was sure that Jane's self-esteem was going to be boosted forever by this little victory, just as mine was by completing the London Marathon.

Wendy was a twenty-something big girl when she first came running, but very quickly she began to lose some weight. She loved it. She was dead keen. Never missed a session. Bought all the gear. And after a few months of this she went into work one day and someone said to her, 'Do you mind if I ask you a personal question?'

'Go on then,' she replied.

'Well... erm... are you having an affair?'

Wendy had been with her husband for fifteen years. Things had settled down into a bit of routine, as they do, but she had no intention of cheating on him. 'You what?' she gasped at her colleague.

'Well, you've changed. You've got a spring in your step that I haven't seen for a long while.'

'I've been going to this running club, that's all,' Wendy laughed.

The colleague was not laughing. She was dead serious when she asked, 'What club is this? Can I join?'

Wendy got home after work intending to go out with three other couples on their monthly night out in Liverpool, but two of the couples had cancelled. When that happened, they usually postponed until the next month.

'Shall we still go?' Wendy's husband Greg asked her.

'What, just me and you?' Wendy couldn't imagine going out on a 'date' like that, just her and Greg. They hadn't done something like that in ages.

But Greg was keen, he loved spending time with this new Wendy with the spring in her step. 'Yeah, why not?'

Wendy went upstairs and put on a pair of jeans. Nothing fancy or trendy, in fact they were dead old, but she felt a million dollars because she hadn't been able to get into them in years.

They went into town and they laughed and laughed and laughed all night. After catching the train home, they got off at their station where you have to walk up a load of steps to the exit. Wendy legged it up the stairs, as if the theme from *Rocky* was blasting out of the station speakers that usually only tell you how delayed the next train is, and she bounced about at the top, fists raised in the air.

Greg stood at the bottom of the stairs looking up at her. He was welling up as he called up, 'Wend, it's amazing. Look at you!'

Katherine was a majestic sixty-three years old when she first came to the club. She wouldn't mind me saying she looked a bit the worse for wear because she'd been worrying about and looking after her husband Ray, who'd had bowel cancer, but he was coming out the other side of it now, and she realised it was time to look after herself too. After a few weeks of running I said to her, "Ere, you're looking great. Have you lost weight?'

'Well, I've gone down a dress size, but the scales don't say I've lost anything.'

'That's just it,' I told her. 'You gain muscle by running and that weighs more than fat, so it's your dress size that shows you you're getting slimmer. Sod what the scales say.'

'Oh I see,' she said, but she had something more exciting to tell me. 'Anyway, Ray said the sparkle has come back in my eye. He's over the moon about me running.'

And then there was Keels. She... Well, perhaps it's about time I shut my gob for a change and let some more of these amazing ladies tell you their own stories.

II

KEELS

Confidence has never been my strong point. Even as I write this I'm wracked with doubt that anyone will like it. Why would anyone be interested in what I have to say? I'm no author and there'll be hundreds of people lining up to tell me just that. Tell me how rubbish I am. Tell me how this is not important or even necessary.

I thought the same way in the early seventies when I was twelve and I first got a guitar. In the safety of my bedroom I would pick it up and strum along to my favourite bands – The Moody Blues, Be Bop Deluxe, The Stranglers, Bauhaus and King Crimson. I dreamed of being on stage like Bob Dylan or Adam Ant, playing songs that I'd written myself, but I never dared step out of my room with the guitar. Being a musician, being in a band, was a man's game – unless you were as dynamic and strong as Debbie Harry or Siouxsie Sioux, who I watched in awe on *Top of the Pops* on a Thursday night, sitting cross-legged on our brown shag-pile carpet with my face almost pressed up against the TV screen.

You only had to look at my family to know that I was right about it being a man's game. My dad played blues harmonica in the local folk clubs and my brother, who was just a year older, played guitar in all sorts of bands, even backing Toyah, another one of those striking female performers I could never compete with.

The music scene in Merseyside at that time was brilliant. Echo & the Bunnymen, A Flock of Seagulls, Teardrop Explodes, OMD, China Crisis, Frankie Goes To Hollywood, The Mighty Wah! and Dead or Alive all emerged from it, particularly from Eric's, a venue on Matthew Street right opposite the Cavern Club. But these groups weren't interested in Merseybeat and living in the shadow of The Beatles. They were determined to shake things up and break away from the stereotypes of Liverpool music. I loved every minute of it. It was as if the Mersey flowed with music not water. And I wanted to dive in.

But, musically speaking, I felt like the ugly duckling of our family. I sometimes wondered if I must have been a great disappointment to them. After all, it was such a musical family, they even named me after the great American jazz singer Keely Smith, but I was pretty sure I never sounded as sweet as her. And so the guitar would stay propped up against my bedroom wall, which was covered in posters of Donny Osmond and pictures I'd ripped out of *Motorcycle News*, for a year or two before I would dare to pick it up again, the beautiful wooden curves of the body covered in dust, just like my voice.

When I left school in the late seventies, I struggled to find work. I'm no divvy but unemployment was on the rise. A wage dispute between Labour Prime Minister James Callaghan and the unions started the Winter of Discontent, when streets were lined with litter, some dead went unburied and parents rushed to feed their own ill children in hospital as everyone from rubbish collectors to grave diggers and nurses went out on strike. In the early eighties, unemployment levels shot up even more and I was out of work until 1988 when I signed up with Her Majesty's Prison Service.

For someone who wouldn't say boo to an ugly duckling, let alone a goose, it seems an unlikely job choice. But it wasn't really a choice. I couldn't go on being unemployed forever and there was an ad in the paper for a job as a prison officer. I applied and was sent to Ashford Remand Centre, which was a bit of shock. I thought I would be going to a women's prison somewhere near Liverpool, but Ashford was all male and on the outskirts of London. It was one of the first years that the prison service started 'cross-sex posting' – prison patter for sending women officers to male prisons and vice versa. And that wasn't the only bit of lingo I picked up in there. From Almond Rocks to Disco Biscuits I soon became fluent. It was an eye-opener I can tell you. I was terrified for my first year, but then thankfully the prison was shut down and I was transferred to Holloway Women's Prison in North London.

At Holloway they sent me to college one day a week to get qualifications in painting and decorating so I could then run a class for some of the inmates. It turned out the four or five girls in my class were the ones considered the hardest to handle. I'm not sure why they were given to me – probably because I didn't have the guts to refuse to have them. But I treated them with respect and they did the same to me. Most of them were glad to be doing something, to have something to get up for, learning a skill they could use when they got out. So the classes were generally fun, which was just as well in a place stuffed full of potentially dangerous women.

But the prison also had its fair share of dishy male officers. I soon fell for one called Pat and we got married in 1996. A couple of years later we had our daughter, who loved nothing more than sightseeing around London sitting in her little backpack strapped to Pat or me. One of the first places we took her was to watch the London Marathon.

I was amazed at the endless stream of runners passing by. I heard the crowd cheering every one of them like they were rock stars. I felt a buzz just watching. Imagine what it would be like to actually run it! I stood there dreaming of completing the marathon just as I used to dream of being a musician. And just as I used to dream of being a musician, I knew that running a marathon would never be a reality for someone like me. I lit up another cigarette and took a lungful of nicotine to console myself.

The year 2000. A brand new century. Everyone was looking to the future, especially me and Pat as we delivered our second child, our son into the world. Pat had to retire early on medical grounds, so we decided to relocate back to the Wirral, to be near my parents for support as we now had two kids to take care of.

Out in the wide world there were fears of impending doom as everyone was going on about 'Y2K', fearing that computers would not shift from 1999 to 2000 correctly and all manner of disasters would befall us because of it. This 'millennium bug' was expected to cause global chaos, with aeroplanes falling out of the sky, missiles firing by accident and the world plunging into darkness. But as the New Year came and went everything went on as usual. Everything was fine.

Except, it seemed, for me.

Trying to assimilate into civilian life back in the north-west was not as easy as I had thought it would be. It was as if I had my own little millennium bug lurking inside of me and, unlike Y2K, it did get triggered.

After twelve years working every day in prisons, you have a very different sense of humour to most mums at the school gates in the Wirral and a whole different set of life experiences. As I stood there looking at all the other women chatting away, I was convinced they didn't want anything to do with me. I was convinced no one wanted to speak to me. That I wasn't good enough for them. I thought I was the lowest of the low. Bottom of the pile of humanity. A waste of space. I was not important and had nothing worth saying. It was that lack of confidence bubbling up again that I could trace back to hiding away in my bedroom strumming my guitar and singing so quietly because I didn't think I was good enough to be heard. My insecurity, my lack of confidence, was my millennium bug. And when it was triggered, aeroplanes did fall out of the sky, missiles did fire by accident, at least in my world. I was plunged into the darkness of a deep depression. A clinical depression. And the doctor prescribed me a course of antidepressants.

Like everyone else on the planet, it seems, I retreated to the virtual world as the real world got too much. I spent hours flicking through Facebook and made myself even more depressed looking at everyone's carefully composed photos of their perfect lives. Until I stumbled on this post from a friend of a friend of a friend called Rachel. I thought she was talking about Jesus or something at first, going on about this epiphany she'd had, this amazing feeling while out running. How she'd gone from an overweight wreck to something resembling human again. How she'd been prescribed Prozac, but had found better results with her drug of choice, running. There were dozens of comments from all sorts of women who were as touched by her words as I had been. And she seemed to be starting some kind of club for other mums who wanted to feel what she had felt. I was one of those mums.

I was terrified she'd tell me to get lost, that this club wasn't for the likes of me, but at least I could hide behind the internet as I messaged her for details of the first session. To my surprise, she said of course I should come along. Be outside the school at 7 p.m. on Wednesday!

When I got near to the school, I could see this woman in bright running gear looking at her watch and pacing about. It had to be Rachel.

I took a deep breath and walked over. 'I'm not late am I?' I said, my voice shaking a bit with nerves.

'No. No, you're right on time,' she said with a reassuring giggle. 'I'm Rachel.'

'Keely,' I said, 'but everybody calls me Keels.'

'Nice to meet you Keels.'

And then two more women arrived. And then another. And before I knew it there were ten of us all looking awkwardly at each other and expectantly at Rachel.

I was rubbish, lagging behind at the back the whole way. But Rachel managed to make it enjoyable. God knows how. And so I actually kept at it. Came back week after week until one day Rachel suggested we all do the London Marathon.

'No, no, no,' I laughed. 'Me? Never.'

'Why not?' Rachel said, and she was utterly serious.

'Well… I'm no good. Look at the state of me.'

'What do you mean, no good?' her sister Lynne said.

'You're as good as the rest of us,' Rachel said, telling me off for even daring to think otherwise.

'I can barely keep up with you lot.'

'But it's not the finish time, it's the finish line,' she smiled as she said one of her favourite mantras. 'And you always finish, don't you?'

'Well...' It was one of my dreams to do the Marathon. And here was someone telling me I could actually do it. The thought was overwhelming. 'But I've got fallen arches.'

'And I've got hidradenitis suppurativa,' Rachel said.

'You what. What's that?'

'I'll explain later, but it's worse than fallen arches, trust me, love.'

'Well...'

'I don't think I can do it, if you don't,' Rachel said with a twinkle in her eye. 'You're an important part of this group. As important as anyone else here.'

Me? Important? I couldn't believe what I was hearing.

'If you don't give it a go, you'll never know,' Clare sang one of her favourite mantras too.

'Well...'

The girls were pleading with me to enter. I couldn't remember the last time I felt so wanted.

'OK. I'll give it a go.'

It seemed impossible enough running a marathon, but what about raising the money needed to enter as a charity runner?

My brother knew a musician from the circuit, a guy called Henry Priestman, who happened to have been chief songwriter and original member of The Christians – a multimillion, Number 1 album-selling, international chart hit band band from Liverpool, who were constantly in the top ten in the late eighties. He suggested we get Henry and his musical partner Les Glover to perform at the Lever Club and charge people to come in support of the charity I would be running for. Henry and Les graciously agreed and, being a couple of local celebrities, we raised the entire amount I needed in that one night.

As I ran up Pall Mall on 26 April 2015, I was fifty-five years old. It had taken me seven and a half hours so far. It felt like London was closing up for the night. The race marshals were just behind me clearing away all the railings, the cheering crowds which they once held back all long gone. Rachel had finished hours ago but, no matter how knackered she must have been, she came back and was there for the last mile running with me, screaming and hollering at me to keep going:

'DIG IN! DIG IN!'

I loved her for doing it, but right then I could have turned round and belted her – if only I had the energy.

But it wasn't just Rachel. All sorts of people were squealing at me, cheering hysterically, as if they were watching two gold medallists battling it out neck and neck near the finish line of the Olympic 1500 metres or something. And I felt like an Olympian as they put that medal round my neck. I had completed the London Marathon. I couldn't believe it, but I'd done it. For the first time in my life I knew for a fact it was possible to make a dream a reality.

I'd kept in touch with Henry Priestman. We became good friends, and back in the Wirral I often went out to watch him play. Many of his songs spoke straight to my heart. I recognised some songs from The Christians days, but it was when he performed one of his solo songs that I was truly captivated because of the lyric which said:

Beautiful dreamers everywhere,
Don't give up, you're nearly there.

It could've been the soundtrack to that last mile I ran of the marathon. And it ignited that feeling that I could do anything again. That I could make my dreams come true. And my biggest dream had always been to be a musician.

'Well,' I told myself, channelling the confidence Rachel and Mums to Marathons had instilled in me, 'I've got something to say, I'm a human being, why shouldn't I get up there too? I can do this.'

For the next year or so, having given up the fags and the antidepressants, I worked on my voice with the help of local musician Kellyann Lea, I polished up my guitar skills with guidance from guitar teacher Skeet Williams, and honed my songwriting. Then, one night, I felt the time had come. I went to the Bromborough Folk Club, a Merseyside musical institution for over thirty years. It was a mecca for me and for many other folk fans and established musicians alike. My dad went every week without fail – still does.

When I took the stage there, I had less control over my legs than I did after twenty-six miles running around London. But I plugged in my guitar. I tapped the mic. I opened my mouth. And…

…I made another dream come true.

12

LESLEY

I owned a hairdresser's in Liverpool and we needed to expand, so we opened another on the Wirral. I moved over with the husband Lee and the kids, but when I got there I thought, 'Oh God, they're just a load of old wools here. Plastic scousers.'

Our shop was on the border of Bebington and Rock Ferry and they all had their heads stuck up their arses there, they all thought they were better than everyone else and then in comes me – rent-a-gob – doing customers' hair, effing and blinding as I do, telling it how it is and they're all looking at me with their jaws on the floor. One day, Lee, who'd stopped by the shop for a cuppa, is going to me, 'Les, you can't really speak to people like that round here. You're not in Liverpool anymore, like?'

'I can fucking do what I want,' I told him. 'They're not here for me personality, they're here for me hair-cutting skills, do you know what I mean?'

Anyway, one of the few customers who didn't have a rod stuck up her arse was telling me about this running club she'd started going to.

'I used to run now and then,' I told her. 'I was always a sporty type, me, going to the gym and that.'

Lee almost spat his tea out.

'Don't look at me like that, you nobhead!' I told him. 'We met in a gym.'

'I don't remember that,' he said.

'Yers don't remember what you had for breakfast this morning, so you can shut your gob.' I turned back to my customer and went, 'But I get bored easily, me. I always start things but I never finish them.'

'If you come to this club, I guarantee you won't get bored,' she grinned.

'Blimey, what is it?' I goes. 'Running with those love balls jammed up your fanny?'

Lee went white.

'Well, if people don't like it they shouldn't be listening in on me convoes, should they?' I told him.

'No,' this girl laughed, 'but somehow this Rachel gets you to do things you never thought you could.'

''Ere, our Lee, you should go along. There's plenty of things I want you to do that I wouldn't think you can, but none of them have got to do with running.'

He wasn't impressed and he showed me.

'Look, he's giving me the finger,' I told my customer. 'Shame it's never when or where I want it.'

When she could get a word in edgeways again, the customer went, 'Come along if you can. I promise you the weight drops off.'

'Well, I've got a bit of a fat arse,' I shouted over the hairdryer. 'But that's trendy nowadays what with Kim Kardashian and that, isn't it?'

I looked at my body in the mirror as I finished blow-drying the customer's hair. I always told everyone that curvy girls were the best, but what woman doesn't want to be a size fucking zero really? Who doesn't want to lose a few pounds? Besides, I was in my mid-forties. I wasn't getting any younger and I could do with getting fitter, for my heart and lungs if not my belly.

So I went, 'All right. I'll give it a go. Why not? When and where?'

And she goes, 'You just turn up outside the school. 7 p.m. Wednesday night.'

So I showed up outside the school at 7 p.m. like my customer told me to. I couldn't believe how many women were there. Thirty? Forty? God knows. Everyone was in their running gear, all chattering away. Now I don't get intimidated that easily, but this was bigger than I'd imagined it, so I quickly scanned the crowd and spotted not just the customer who'd invited me but loads of other customers too. I got chatting to them and then I was away. There were some la-di-da ones, proper Wirral posh, like. One of them was moaning about married life, how she's often making a pavlova with one hand and doing the laundry with the other.

So I chimed in, 'As long as you don't get the two mixed up. Don't want creamy knickers.'

And then this other woman sniggered, 'Chance'd be a fine thing.'

That's my kind of girl, I was saying to myself, and then the same girl starts telling us all how to stretch, how to breathe and I realise she's this Rachel who leads the club. She gravitated towards me because she liked to look after the newbies apparently and she starts chatting as we run. Well, it's been a few years since I've done more than run a bath, so I've barely got enough breath to stay alive, let alone chat.

'Jesus, Rachel, don't you ever shut up, like?' I said, after we'd come to the next lamppost she was using as markers.

And she goes, 'I wish I'd had someone chatting to me when I started running, to keep my mind off how bloody far I had left to go.'

So I went, 'And how far have we got left to go?' I was panting more than I'd done in the bedroom in years.

'Well, we've done two miles,' Rachel grinned.

'Two miles?' I screeched. 'How the fuck did that happen?' I was absolutely made up.

The next thing I knew Rachel's talking about 10Ks and bloody marathons.

'Swerve that!' I thought. I don't mind jogging a couple of miles now and then, but I was buggered if I was going to commit to all that time training, eating right, not to mention the chafing. I've heard stories about the marathon: I don't fancy having my nipples bleed, thank you very much. The only marathon I'd be doing would be a twenty-six-mile pub crawl.

But anyway, me and Rachel soon became thick as thieves. As we ran, we talked, and she told me all about her unhappy marriage. I felt for her and I realised how lucky I was with our Lee. We did stuff together but we did stuff apart too and we never got paranoid about it. Trevor on the other hand sounded like a total twat.

She phoned me in a state once when he'd done something particularly twatish. That proper boiled my piss.

So I went, 'I'm coming round there, and I'll knock ten types of shit out of the wanker.'

'Ey, ey, ey, slow down there, Les!' our Lee said, ever the diplomat. 'Let's just invite her round here for a break and a chat. We don't have to go around there causing more trouble for her.'

So we invited her round and she poured her heart out, but the more she told me the more protective I felt about her. And the more protective I got the more I felt like opening my gob, so of course I did. And as I started telling Rachel what a proper nobhead I thought Trevor was, she would start defending him.

'Yeah but he's still my husband. He's still the father of my children. I don't wish anything bad for him.'

You could tell she was uncomfortable. Lee shut me up with a well-timed glare which made me realise we were embarrassing her. Telling her what a shitty relationship she was in. Who wants to hear that? If *she* wanted to bitch about him, she could, but no one else was allowed to. I got it. That's just how I would be about my Lee. We were making her feel attacked, making her feel like a mug for staying in that marriage. She didn't need that from us. She needed support. We changed the subject to running. That always cheered her up.

So I told her what a tit she was for training for the London Marathon.

'Are you sure you don't want to do it with us, love?' Rachel smiled. It was good to see her smiling again.

'Fuck off! I'll come and support though. Hold the handbags and the gin. There's plenty of pubs on the route, like, isn't there?'

Lee piped up, 'Ey, you always talked about doing a sports massage course, Les.' He had all the time in the world for Mums to Marathons, because he had not only seen what it had done for me, he had made a load of new friends among the husbands whenever we got together for a social. 'Why don't you become the club's official physio, like,' he grinned.

'Oh yeah,' I went. 'You've got a point there. If there's one thing these nutters are going to need after twenty-six miles, it'll be a good dose of physio.'

Rachel was made up about that idea so that tipped the balance for me. I enrolled on a course and did all my practical training on the Mums to Marathons girls. My house turned into a fucking massage parlour. What with all the girls coming and going so I could practise on them, and their moans and groans like they were having a fucking orgasm as I sorted out their knotted muscles, I'm surprised the neighbours didn't call the pigs and tell them I was running a house of ill repute.

13

RUMBLINGS

Lesley was giving me a massage. 'Ooh, right there, yeah,' I moaned.

'Can I watch?' Lee shouted from the kitchen.

'Fuck off!' we both said in unison.

'Concentrate on cooking the tea,' Lesley called out then said to me, 'Fuck me there's some knots in there, Rach.'

'Running myself ragged with the clubs all over the place now, arn' I,' I told her.

'But running is supposed to be good for you, love, not draining.'

'Oh, don't get me wrong, Les, it is good for me. It's the only time I feel alive. The only time I can get my thoughts in order, like.'

'But…?' she said.

'You what?'

'I'm feeling a but,' Lesley said, 'and I don't mean this one.' She slapped my arse.

I laughed, just as Lesley hoped I would, but she wanted to hear what was on my mind too. She wasn't going to let me off the hook that easily. So I told her.

I told her how one of the girls called Polly, who'd run with us since the Bebington club had started, had always been dropped off by her husband at the school gates where we gathered at the start of each session. Me, being me, I always bounded over and said hello to her husband, Ian, as Polly got out of the car, but it was like he couldn't bring himself to even look at me let alone speak to me. If he did look, it was more of a glare and nothing more than a resentful nod. I didn't think too much of it. Just put it down to him being a grumpy bugger, but I couldn't help noticing that Polly was very subdued as she got out of the car and there was no goodbye between them, no see you later, no kiss, nothing. But as soon as he'd driven off and Polly had watched his car drive out of sight, she came alive. She loved every minute of our sessions. She chatted away when we weren't running and, when we were, she breathed in with her eyes almost closed as if she was smelling fresh air for the first time. It all rang a bell the size of Big Ben to me: the look on Ian's face, his ignorance, Polly's transformation from depressed little mouse to a leaping gazelle like you see on a David Attenborough programme when he'd gone. She was just like me and he was just like Trevor.

'Everything alright, love,' I said to Polly one day as she started to shrivel up again, waiting for Ian to pick her up.

'Yeah, just knackered.'

'Is Ian alright?'

'What do you mean?' she said, a little guarded now.

'With you running and that.'

She took a deep breath, held it as she looked up at the night sky, then said, 'Oh, you know, he gets a bit of a cob on when I do this. He doesn't see the point. Thinks I'm wasting my time.'

'Thinks you should be at home chained to the kitchen sink?' I said.

She nodded.

'Thinks you're a bad mother if he has to put the kids to bed once in a while?'

She laughed, but there was no joy in it. It was a laugh of sad recognition.

'Don't worry, love. You're not alone.'

But Ian wasn't the only one who had a problem with the club. There were rumblings that a few of the husbands were not happy with their partners joining Mums to Marathons either.

After I told all this to Lesley, she was fuming. 'Who is it?'

'What do you mean?'

'What husbands? Tell me and I'll go round to each one with a fucking baseball bat and kneecap the little shits.'

'No, no, don't worry, Les. It's just gossip. It won't come to anything, like.'

'It better not, the little tossers.'

'Not everyone's as sound as your Lee, are they?' I sighed.

'Hmm,' Lesley grumbled. 'Want me to do your front, love?'

'I definitely want to see that,' Lee called out from the kitchen.

'Fuck off!' we shouted and cracked up.

It must have been only a day or two later that I was having a little drink down the pub with our Lynne and Lew. Mum was looking after the kids. Trevor had come too, but he was chatting to Pete and some other lads by the pool table, when over by the bar I spotted Matt. When I say spotted, you couldn't bloody miss him. Six foot three and hugely overweight, a mountain of a bloke, he was a bit of a local character, popular, did a lot for the local youth. Him and a group of about five other blokes were standing in a circle mumbling amongst themselves and they kept looking over at our table. When Lew had gone off to the little boys' room I whispered to our Lynne:

'Ey, am I being paranoid or does Matt and his lot keep looking at me?'

'I don't know, Rach,' Lynne said but she kept an eye on them for the next few minutes and then she whispered, 'You're right, they are.'

'One of them's mates with that Ian, you know, Polly's husband.'

'From M2Ms?'

I nodded. 'I think they've got a problem with the club.'

'What club?' Lew said as he sat back down.

'Mums to Marathons.'

'Who has?'

'Them lot,' Lynne nodded as subtly as she could towards the bar.

'Nah!' Lew said draining his pint. 'Why would anyone have a problem with you lot running? Another round?'

Lynne and I nodded and Lew went to the bar. No sooner had he started giving his order, Matt and his cronies thought it was safe to come over and start trouble. He stood over our table blocking out all the light with his mates peeking out from behind him.

'Little cowards,' I thought, but my heart was going like the clappers.

''Ere, Rachel,' Matt boomed.

'What?' I sneered.

'This little running club of yours.'

I knew it! 'Yeah? What about it?'

'I've been hearing a lot about it, you know what I mean, like?'

'No, I don't know what you mean, Matt. Tell me!'

'Well, Gazza here says his wife is at it twice a week.'

'Lucky Gazza,' Lew said bringing back the drinks.

Lynne gave him a hard slap on the leg and told him to shush.

'Running twice a week that is,' Matt clarified.

'Yeah, well,' I said, 'that's how you get the benefit from running, doing it regularly, Matt.'

'Well… then there's Eddie here,' Matt said, slinging his thumb over the opposite shoulder to the one Gazza was hiding behind. 'He says you take the girls out in all weathers.'

'Yes, Matt, they're grown-ups. They can handle a bit of rain.'

'And Jez reckons he hardly recognises his wife since she's been doing the running thing with you.'

'What, do you forget what she looks like if she goes out for a couple of hours twice a week, Jez? Messes with your head if she's not behind the kitchen sink when you come in from work?' I was fuming.

'No, no,' Jez piped up. 'It's great that she's unrecognisable.'

'Ey?' I said.

'Yeah, she was a miserable old cow before.'

'So what's your problem, lads?' I said loudly so the rest of the pub could here. 'What's wrong with your wives going and getting fit, getting healthy – mentally and physically – and having a bit of fun at the same time, ey?'

Matt held his hands up at my little tirade. 'Nothing, nothing, it's just…'

'Just what, *Matt*?' I noticed how his name rhymed with twat.

'It's just we were wondering,' he stuttered, 'if you, like if you don't mind, if you could... well... do a club for us, you know what I mean?'

'Us?'

'Yeah, the lads.' He blushed.

I heard Lew and Lynne giggle as Matt went on, 'You've done wonders for them, so we thought you might be able to help us too. But you know, if it's too much trouble, like.' He turned to Gazza and mumbled, 'I knew we shouldn't have come over.'

I could feel a massive grin slowly spread across my face. It was a grin of relief as much as anything, but it was also one of excitement for a new challenge.

And so the Hub Club was born. I would run with my Bebington girls from 6:30 p.m. to 7:30 p.m. and then the boys from 7:30 p.m. to 8:30 p.m. Then I would have to decide which of the other M2Ms clubs around the Wirral I could get to in the week and which I couldn't. I was running four nights a week, but still I couldn't get to them all. I really wanted to, and I felt a pressure to, because if I didn't go the girls would begin to complain that they didn't feel motivated to carry on. If anyone had dropped out simply because I wasn't there enough, I would have been gutted. I would have failed them, and there was no way I was going to let that happen.

14

THE MARRAKESH MONSOON

'I've got this burning desire to do something big again,' I said.

Lesley groaned, even though I was the one on the massage table. 'Bigger than leading all these clubs all over the Wirral? And God knows how many on the same night? Christ, you need your head examined, you do,' she said.

'It has been, many times. The doctors don't know what to make of it,' I laughed.

'Oh, don't, love.'

'Seriously. Mark, you know, the events manager at Claire House Children's Hospice, he suggested trekking the Sahara.'

Les yelped, 'The Sahara Desert?'

I hummed my yes into the pillow.

'I hope you told him to do one,' she said.

'No, I told him to sign me up!'

'You what?'

'I just blurted it out without a second thought. I think it's exactly the kind of challenge I was craving. I just didn't know it until Mark suggested it.'

'You're fucking barmy, like.'

'Well, we know that, but are you coming?' I looked up, grinning.

Les was knocked off-kilter a bit. She thought for a moment, then said, 'How many days?'

'Ten.'

'Fuck off! Running?'

'No, you nobhead, trekking, walking.'

Lesley looked at me for a second and then a grin spread across her face too. 'The Sahara Desert? I've always dreamed about going there actually.' She pondered for another couple of seconds – seconds which seemed to go on forever. And then she said the words I was dying to hear. 'Fuck it. Go on then.'

Lynne signed up too and within a few days Mums to Marathons had taken every one of the thirty places available on the trip. It would mean a lot of fundraising to cover the costs and provide much-needed donations to the hospice, but we were all so excited to go, nothing was going to stand in our way and it wasn't long before we'd raised all the funds we needed.

The night we were leaving we gathered outside the pub to catch the coach down to London, from where we'd fly to Morocco. All the husbands and kids were there saying goodbye to their wives, their mums. Hugs and kisses all round, except for me of course. Trevor was there, but he just leant against the wall of the pub looking down his nose at it all. He looked like the last person on earth who would be offering up a kiss or a hug to his wife right then, so I started to get on the coach without even thinking of saying goodbye to him.

Then I stopped halfway up the steps.

'You've got to say goodbye to him,' I told myself. 'Don't be as bad as him. He's probably just waiting for you to reach out, for you to make the first move, then he'll get over himself.'

'Are you getting on or what? You're blocking the way, nobhead,' Lesley said, jiggling about with excitement as if she were dying for a wee.

'Sorry, love,' I said, coming out of my trance.

I got off the bus again and went and gave Trevor a hug. 'See you then.'

Nothing. He didn't put his arms around me in return. He didn't say a word. Not even so much as a bon voyage, and where I was going I might well be needing it. But he couldn't care less.

'You all right, our Rach?' said Lynne as I plonked myself next to her on the coach.

'I could be going to Timbuktu for all he cares.'

'Oh, love,' she said putting her arm around me.

'I think we are,' Lesley said, looking at her *Rough Guide*.

'You what?' Lynne said.

'Look! Timbuktu. It's in the bloody Sahara.'

In the Travelodge in London, Lynne was already sleeping soundly next to me and I envied her for it. I wouldn't be sleeping anytime soon. My mind was racing. Funny phrase that, your mind is racing. What's it trying to beat? If it's sleep, then it was bloody well winning that night. I suppose they mean it's the thoughts that race through the mind rather than the mind itself doing the racing. And my mind was like the streets of London during the Marathon, with thousands upon thousands of thoughts running through it, some hopeful, some waving at the crowd with a grin, some with looks of determination, others with pained expressions, some downright doubled over in agony. Most were thoughts of Trevor and the way he'd leaned up against that pub wall as if he was propping it up, looking after it in case it might fall down, when that was all I ever wanted him to do for me.

I know relationships are a two-way street. That's why I went and gave him a hug, made the first move if you like, gave him a chance to show his love without having to get over the embarrassment of hugging me first, you know, just in case it felt difficult for him – men are often rubbish at showing their feelings, that way, I told myself. But putting your arms around someone who is hugging you, no matter how much you don't want to, is almost instinctive isn't it, man or woman. To not return a hug, that takes some effort. That takes some premeditated coldness especially when you know a lot of other people are watching. That's a statement. But what was he stating? What was the message he was trying to convey? Was I missing something? Was I being stupid? Was he trying to tell me what a bad wife I was being, going off galivanting round the world when he needed me by his side? Was he trying to tell me what a bad mother I was being, leaving my kids for ten days so I could have the trip of a lifetime? All the effort I put into raising the money to go, perhaps I should have been putting that into raising my kids. I wished I could have gone out for a run. A run pushes those racing thoughts down to your feet. Like dirty lumps of coal are burnt to fire pistons that move to make electricity that lights our homes and warms our bones, so ugly clusters of thoughts can be turned into movement as we pound the streets, movement that energises the body, movement that's meditative and heals the mind. But it was the middle of the night. I didn't know my way round the streets outside the hotel and this was the Big scary Smoke not little leafy Bebington. If it wasn't for the image of all those other husbands and kids cheering their wives and mothers on as we drove off from the pub that morning, if it wasn't for Lesley's Lee and their kids, and our Lynne's Lew being so supportive of them, I would have never slept that night, believing I was the issue, I was the problem in our marriage, and I would've been packing my case and looking for a train back to Liverpool right then and there. But I didn't. I held onto that image as if it were a lifebuoy as an ocean of darker images tried to pull me under.

The next morning, me almost feeling hungover after all the tossing and turning, we were winging our way from London to Marrakesh. The sheer excitement of it all kept me going. The check-in, the take-off, the flight, the landing, the piling onto a coach and heading into a country and a continent I'd never set foot on before. We were to spend one night in a hotel in Marrakesh either side of the trek, but when we tumbled off the coach and inside off the noisy dusty street, the shock of what we saw finally brought me to a standstill.

'Bloomin 'eck,' said Lynne. 'Look at this place!'

'I thought it was supposed to be a three star hotel.'

'It's meant to be,' I whispered.

To us it looked more like a five star one. We all stood with our gobs wide open in the foyer. It was so ornate. Stained glass above the doors, high ceilings, a fountain in the middle. It was churchlike. Or perhaps mosque-like since we were in a country where over ninety-nine per cent of the population were Muslim, according to Lesley's guide book. But I had no idea – I'd never been in a mosque in my life.

'Look at all this!' Lynne said admiring the deep blue tiles that covered the floor and crept up the columns too.

'Whoever did this can come and do my bathroom,' Lesley said. 'My Lee's fucking hopeless with grouting.'

We made the most of the comfy beds – I was pretty sure we wouldn't be this comfortable for the next eight nights – and I slept like a log at last.

Shortly after dawn the next day, we piled into several jeeps and set off for the desert where the trek would begin. The drive was incredible. None of us had seen anything like it before.

'The farthest I've ever been is bloody Benidorm,' Lesley said, her nose pressed up against the window.

I'd been all over south-east Asia and Japan when I was dancing, but I'd never been to Africa. I was as gobsmacked as the rest, as we bounced our way through the Atlas Mountains on roads which clung to the sides of cliffs with sheer drops on the outside and not a crash barrier in sight.

'How the fuck did anyone build a road up here?' Lesley said, staring out at the barren landscape.

The mountains we drove up looked like something from Mars, and in the distance there were even greater mountains, snow-capped and blue.

After seven hours of driving we were all exhausted, but the novelty of the adventure kept us going until we were dropped off at the mouth of the desert.

'The mouth of the desert?' our Lynne said. 'Sounds a bit ominous, doesn't it? Like it's going to swallow us whole.'

'Come on, girls!' I said, trying to keep everyone's spirits up. 'This is where the real adventure starts.'

The jeeps disappeared and were replaced with a small herd of annoyed-looking camels led by some Moroccan men, who looked the opposite of annoyed. The camels would carry a lot of the gear and food. We walked fifteen miles through scrubland. Nothing looked like my image of the Sahara – rolling sand dunes, blue skies and a dishy Omar Sharif riding towards me through the heat haze on the back of a camel. It wasn't even that hot. The skies were cloudy, it looked as if it might rain at any second.

'Are you sure we're in the Sahara?' Lesley asked, scowling at the sky. 'It looks like a bank holiday in Birkenhead.'

But then, out of nowhere, these massive dunes rose from the scrub. Creamy, rippling sand as far as the eye could see. Our guides pointed up and we realised we had to trek over these steep monsters. Every time we put one foot forward it would slide back into the sand. It was like being on a cross trainer.

'At least my arse should get firmer, doing this,' Lesley cackled.

'Come on, come on,' we shouted at each other, 'you can do it!'

We eventually made it to the top of a dune, exhausted and curling up with laughter. Our guides led us along the peak. I felt like I was walking a tightrope between the sunny and shaded sides of the mountain of sand, which snaked on endlessly, but I walked without fear. I was elated. It was beautiful, a dreamscape, despite the clouds which still hung in the sky.

We camped that night in very basic two-man tents, a far cry from the hotel back in Marrakesh – each tent nothing more than a piece of tatty canvas slung over a few poles. Our guides started digging trenches all around our camp, which was weird and we couldn't really get to the bottom of why they were doing it. Many things got lost in translation, so I just trusted they were doing whatever was best for us.

'Perhaps it's to keep wild animals out,' said Lynne.

'Who invited her along?' Lesley grumbled.

'I'm sure everything's fine,' I said, not quite believing what I was saying. 'Now I don't know about you lot but I'm going to lay on my back and look up at the stars.'

That seemed to do the trick. All the girls were distracted by the promise of some of the most stunning night skies the world has to offer.

After a few minutes of silence, Lesley cut through it with: 'Where's the fucking stars then?'

There wasn't a single pinprick of light in the whole of the heavens. It was far too cloudy.

'We should get some sleep,' I suggested. 'We'll need all our energy for tomorrow.'

In the middle of the night I was woken by the sound of something ripping at the tent I was sharing with our Lynne.

It woke her too. 'Bloomin' 'eck, what's that, Rach?'

Perhaps Lynne was right. Perhaps there were wild animals out there. Lynne and I clung to each other eyes wide open, straining into the dark, ears like satellite dishes. And as we listened some more, the sound became more recognisable. It wasn't the terrifying and exotic noise of some desert beast, but something far too familiar to anyone from the north-west of England.

'It can't be what I think it is, can it?'

'It bloody is.'

'Are you sure?'

'Yeah, I'm sure all right. I'm getting soaked here.'

A monsoon's worth of rain was lashing at our tents.

'I told you it was Birkenhead,' we heard Lesley screech from the next-door tent.

'Torrential rain in the Sahara?' one of the other girls squealed.

In the morning, as we wrung out our soaking onesies with *Mums to Marathons on Tour* printed on the back, which we all slept in each night, our guides managed to explain to us that it hadn't rained like this in over twenty years. There had been a flash flood which had swept through the desert a mile and a half away from our position. Now the trenches dug all around the camp made perfect sense. There was something else they were not willing to share with us, we could tell, but I put it down to the language barrier again and looked forward to the day ahead.

We had to change our route a little because of the flooding, but after a few days we were back on track and the skies had cleared so that the nights were as we all had hoped: incredible. At last we could lay on our backs under the stars which filled the sky in ways we had never seen. Everywhere we looked, north, east, south and west, the sky came down to the ground, not a building or even a tree to interfere. We had the sense of being in a humungous snow dome, but it would be stars that fell all around us, not snow, when you shook it. The densest part of the Milky Way dusted the sky directly overhead and there was an utterly magical silence. Except for the little snivels of each of us as we quietly wept at the beauty of it all…

…until a camel let off an enormous fart and we all cackled with joy.

In the mania of that moment I decided we were going to play Off Ground Tick. If you don't know, in Off Ground Tick one person would be 'on' and they would chase everyone else to 'tick' them but if you could lift yourself onto a fence, wall, tree or anything off the ground then you couldn't be caught. In the desert, of course, this was impossible, but that was the point; it just added to the mania and made us laugh even more. There we were racing around like kids, but we were all in our forties and fifties – it was brill.

And in the unlikely event, during all that fun, that we should forget why we were there, every morning Mark from the charity, who had come along on the trip, would read a letter from one of the kids that used the hospice, or even from one of the parents of those kids. Their words of gratitude would invariably have us all in tears, but it made us more determined than ever to carry on. Words like:

Just over five years ago we were given the devastating news that our one-year-old son, Alfie, had a life-limiting condition called Migrating Partial Epilepsy of Infancy, a rare condition affecting just 100 children worldwide. He had constant seizures, sometimes up to 200 every day, and was constantly in and out of hospital. The doctors told us that he would become ill with many complications and that most probably he would not live to see his 5th birthday.

Our world fell apart.

Shortly after receiving this news we were referred to Claire House Hospice and had our first stay back in August 2009. I remember we felt sick to the stomach with nerves, the thought of using a hospice filled us with sadness and with thoughts of endings, and the word I could not bring myself to say in relation to Alfie... death.

We couldn't have been more wrong. We had the best times at Claire House and it became like a second home to us. We would stay at the hospice once every three months or so. Alfie's needs became so complex that each time we walked through the doors for a stay it felt like a huge weight being lifted from our shoulders. Handing over all medications and therapies and just being able to be Mum to Alfie and his older brother Josh for a few days was an amazing feeling. Josh loved his time at the hospice because he was looked after as well as Alfie.

Last year in April, Alfie's condition worsened. We were all exhausted, so were offered a stay at Claire House for some support and to recharge our batteries.

Alfie died in my arms the day after we arrived. He was five years old.

The love, kindness and support we received over the next few days and weeks from the staff was just everything we needed and I honestly don't know how we would have managed without them all. We were able to keep Alfie with us for another six days after he died. We placed him on a bed in the Butterfly Suite and Josh put all his favourite toys around him; we stayed in a bedroom right opposite him so we were close at all times. Family and friends were able to come and say goodbye and for us to have that precious time with Alfie after he died was a gift. Without the hospice this would not have been possible. We were given much-needed help to plan Alfie's funeral by our amazing contact worker Trish. We were helped to put together the order of service and liaise with everyone from the funeral home to the vicar; nothing was too much trouble.

We will be forever grateful to Claire House for the vital help and support during Alfie's short life and in the years since he died.

One night near the end of our ten days, we found ourselves back at the Atlas Mountains. We were to camp at the base of them and this time climb up on foot. When we reached the top, Mark had us sit down facing the awesome desert and asked us to reflect once more on Claire House and the kids and the journey we had taken in their name. I did just that, but I think we all reflected on more than that. On not just the journey we had taken in the name of the kids, but the journey we had taken in our lives. My God, these barren mountains and this desert with its steep dunes and unheard-of flash floods could have been a metaphor for my life so far.

I wept for the beauty in that life. I wept for the tragedy in it too. I wept because I missed my kids and I thanked God they were not in need of a hospice, although I couldn't think of a better place than Claire House to take them if I ever had to. And I wept because in a day or two I would be back home – or rather, in the house I shared with Trevor.

'Right,' said Mark gently, but with a twinkle in his eye. 'Now we have a little surprise.'

He started handing out letters to each of us. We all tore them open eagerly.

'What is it?'

'Oh my God.'

I saw Lynne slap hers to her chest as soon as she'd begun to read it.

'Who's yours from?'

Mark raised his voice over our chatter. 'You each have a letter from your husbands or partners. And if you don't mind, I thought it would be nice to read them all out to each other.'

There were 'Ah's and a few tears already.

'Who wants to start?' Mark scanned the group. 'Lynne?'

'Yes. OK.'

'All right, a bit of hush, ladies!'

We all quietened down as Lynne read out loud:

Hi babe,

Since you've started your Forrest Gump impressions and fundraising for Claire House I've not stopped thinking how proud I am of you and your achievements. From your first 10K to your half marathons and now your Sahara Trek, it's just a million miles away from anything you've done before, it's brilliant. I've always had my golf to get me

124

through tough times and I can see how your running gets you through yours, which is why it's so important you keep going at it. Added to that your legs have never looked so good... sorry couldn't resist.

Keep it going babe and keep that cash rolling in for Claire House.

Missing you more than you know.

All my love

Lew

'Oh my God. What a sweetheart,' Lesley said.

'Who's next?' said Mark.

One of the other girls volunteered, then Lesley read her Lee's funny and loving words, then the rest – all wonderfully emotional messages in their own way. Finally, it was my turn. I was hoping they'd forget about me.

'And last but by no means least,' Mark announced, 'your illustrious leader, Rachel.'

The girls all cheered me, bless them, and I saw the paper quivering in my hand. I thought it was the breeze at first... Well, I hoped it was the breeze, but I knew it was my hands that were trembling. I looked at Mark, he gave me an encouraging smile. My stammer was not a big problem these days – the confidence that I got from running and from Mums to Marathons had done it the power of good – but it came back heavily when I was stressed, tired or nervous. It took me a while to stutter through the letter from Trevor – and I wasn't tired:

Dear Rachel,

I'm not great at writing letters, but I just wanted to say, you setting up Mums to Marathons and raising so much money for the hospice is admirable. The kids and I are very proud of you. You've not only achieved great things for yourself – the London Marathon, for example – but I know that you help many people achieve things they never thought they could.

Enjoy every minute of your trek, but come home safely.

Trevor xx

Everyone cheered and then thanked Mark for making the letters happen. There were group hugs and more tears and then excited chatter as everyone slowly made their way back down the mountain to camp.

'Are you coming, our Rach?'

'Yeah. I'll catch you up.'

I perched on a boulder and called Mark back as he followed the girls down.

'You all right?' he asked.

'That letter from Trevor. Was it really from him?'

Mark almost nodded. He wanted so desperately to say yes, but instead he looked like one of my kids when I catch them with their hands in the biscuit tin.

'It wasn't really from him, was it?'

Mark allowed a lone bird in the sky to catch his attention, so he didn't have to answer me right away.

'It's OK, Mark.'

I began to walk down the mountain.

'Rachel, we tried.'

I stopped and turned back to Mark. He looked ill.

'We asked Trevor. We asked and we asked, so many times. But he never responded.'

'So you wrote it?'

Mark nodded.

'I could tell. It was far too wordy for him.'

15

A ROOM FULL OF BUBBLE WRAP

When the coach pulled up outside the pub again in Bebington there were homemade banners waving, children and husbands cheering. It was a lovely welcome back. My chest filled up like one of the balloons tied to the lamppost, but as I scanned the crowd for Trevor and my kids, my balloon was well and truly popped. They weren't there. I shouldn't have been surprised, given the send-off Trevor gave me. It was just like my first half marathon with Bev and Ally, crossing the line to the same cheers and banners from everyone except my husband who'd stood there with a face like a slapped arse. In a way it was better that he wasn't there, then I could pretend he didn't exist, that this welcome back was exactly the way it was supposed to be, that everyone that was here was exactly who should be here. But the fact that the kids weren't there really stuck in my gut.

Back home, as I unpacked, I should have been chatting away to my husband who should be leaning in the bedroom doorway wanting to know everything. *How was it? What was the desert like? Did you ride a camel? You must be knackered, love. Here, take the weight off, I've made your tea, tell me all about it!* But instead he behaved like I'd just got back from the shops. If the kids ever asked me about my trip, which if course they did, he'd make a point of getting up and stomping into another room so he didn't have to hear about it.

It was late November and, before you knew it, the Christmas party season was in full swing. We always went to Dee and Ollie's party.

'Let's take that bottle of Prosecco with us, Trev.'

'You must be joking. They're posh. I'm not having them look down their noses at us.'

'They're lovely, they don't care what we bring.'

'No, I'm not having that. We'll take that Lidl champagne.'

'Oooh, that'll show them,' I mumbled to my vanity mirror.

Then Sam came into the bedroom saying, 'Dad, can we go to London to watch Tranmere play Liverpool?'

'Oh yeah,' I said taking a pause from doing my lippy. 'They're doing a special package deal on the coach, aren't they? It'll be a nice day out for you both.'

'Why the hell would I go all the way to London to watch Tranmere,' Trevor snapped, stamping his feet into his best shoes, 'when I don't even watch them up here?'

'Trevor,' I said, seeing Sam deflate. 'It's not about you, is it? Sam's mad about Tranmere. It would mean the world to him.'

His only response was, 'Are you ready or what?'

So we went to Dee and Ollie's and, because I hadn't seen them since well before my trip to Morocco, as soon as we walked in they asked me how it had gone. I, of course, started chatting away about it, while Trevor rolled his eyes, as he had done whenever I'd tried to tell him anything about the trip. But I just ignored him. I had loads to tell my friends. I told them about how awesome the dunes were, how beautiful the night sky was, how we laughed and cried, how, Sod's Law, it had rained harder than it had done in over twenty years and caused a flash flood in the desert. I also told them the news that the guides had kept from us after the flood because they didn't want to bring us down on our trip of a lifetime.

'It was really sad,' I said to Dee. 'I found out after we got back to the hotel that the flash flood was so sudden, so severe, that thirty-odd locals lost their lives.'

'Oh my God, that's awful,' Ollie said nearly choking on his vol-au-vent.

'I know,' I said patting him on the back – no Heimlich manoeuvre necessary, thank God. 'They had helicopter rescue teams on standby for us too and it turns out if we had been camping a mile and a half further in, we would have been dead now too.'

That's when Trevor sniped, 'But you *weren't* a mile and a half further in and you're *not* dead, are you?' as if that came as a great disappointment to him.

Ollie, now fully recovered, didn't know where to look.

Dee tried to shift the focus away from what Trevor had said. 'I can't bear to think about what the families of those locals have gone through, but we have to count our blessings that you're back in one piece, don't we?'

My face was red-hot, burning with embarrassment, but I was so angry too. The first thing Dee thought about, God love her, was the families of those that died, but the welfare of Trevor's family, of his wife, seemed to be the last thing he wanted to consider. I couldn't hold it in any longer. I think I shouted. I hope not, but I can't remember – I was lost in such a fog of rage – but the words came blurting out. 'You've always got to put me down, haven't you! Why can't you support me in anything I do? You must really hate me.'

I stormed out of the house. I marched off down the road sobbing my heart out and my feet took me straight to where they needed to go. Home. To my mum's.

She put the kettle on, gave me a hug, you know, those simple little things that mean everything, and after an hour or so I got a text. From Trevor. I opened it up quickly, eagerly, expecting to read an apology, but I must have been off my head to expect that. Instead he said something about having a good time and that no one was missing me at the party. He also said that when people had asked where I was he'd told them my piles were playing me up so I had to go. Nice!

And then a few hours after that when I was back at the house, he sent another text. I opened it with the same stupid eagerness, but he was just asking for a lift home.

You won't be surprised I ignored that text too. And I made sure I was fast asleep – or at least pretended to be – when he stumbled into bed that night. I lay there thinking how this was just like it used to be in Japan. Me pretending to be asleep as Max stumbled, pissed out of his head, into bed. Is this how all my relationships were going to go? Is this the way everyone's relationships go? Should I just accept it as a fact of life? Or just my life?

My mental health was at a real low. None of the girls in Mums to Marathons would even know it. I could act the clown, turn on the jokes and the smiles to keep them all motivated because – at the risk of this sounding like a Miss World speech – when I knew I was helping someone else I was truly happy.

But at the end of the training session I always knew I had to go back to him. I would lie in bed and my mind would be the thing running now, but it wasn't the kind of running that would do it any good. It was stuffed with thoughts, often psychotic images. I tried to explain the feeling to our Lynne and the best way I could was this: imagine your entire living room is stuffed with bubble wrap, every inch of it from ceiling to floor, and someone says go in there and pop every single bubble in one minute or I'm going to kill your kids. It's an impossible task, you know it, but you have to do it. Imagine the terror, how riddled with anxiety you would be! And how that horror would not go away even as you tried your hardest to pop every stupid bubble. That is the kind of anxiety and horror that filled my head every day. A billion thoughts teemed through my mind like a plague of locusts. I needed to work hard at being just OK, where OK is the default setting for most people without depression. I had given up all the shrinks and mental health appointments because I had a great support system in Mums to Marathons – we all did – but that didn't mean I could stop the antidepressants. I realised I didn't feel normal because I was missing certain chemicals in my brain. I didn't feel bad about that anymore. It was just the same as having anaemia and taking a pill to replace the iron missing in your body. But I'd realised the pill couldn't do the whole job. Running completed the prescription. I would take myself for a nice 10K and out there in that spiritual state which running gave me, bathing in the endorphins the exercise produced, I could get a little perspective, bask in the good things in my life instead of dwelling on the bad.

Trevor came in pissed just after Christmas, January 2015. I'd just put Harriet down. It had taken me ages to get her to sleep, but she was off now and so were the boys, so I could flake out on the bed too. I was so desperate to get some sleep but before my mind could switch off I heard the door go and him thudding up the stairs. And then what does he bloody well do? He goes in and wakes the kids up. I was livid. He got Harriet and Ben out on the landing and he was tickling them and they were falling about laughing, thinking he was the best dad in the world. Harriet then wanted to go for a wee and when she was on the toilet she said to Trevor, 'Daddy, I've got a sore twinkle.'

Now, little girls get sore twinkles from time to time. It happens. It's not an indication of poor hygiene or bad parenting. I knew Harriet had got a sore twinkle so I had put some Sudocrem on it and done the usual things a mother does when her daughter is sore down there.

But when she told Trevor, he came into our bedroom and started tearing into me. 'What the fuck is that all about? She shouldn't be sore down there.'

I opened my mouth to speak, but he carried on shouting at me.

'You're a shit mother. You can't even keep the kids clean.'

When I finally got a word in, I gave him what for. 'What the fuck are you talking about? What would you know about bringing these kids up? I do it all. *I* brought these kids up, not you. I do the cleaning, the cooking, the taking them to and fro for their activities. And they are well looked after, no thanks to you. What do you know about how clean they are? When we was kids it was a bath on a Sunday and every other day a top and tail wash. They get showers or baths every bloody day. There's nothing wrong with these kids' hygiene.'

He ignored me and went out to Harriet and Ben, who were still playing on the landing. 'Do you want to come and sleep with Daddy?'

He had never said that to them in his life. They had tried to get in bed with us a million times but he had never allowed it. This was clearly designed just to piss me off.

'Yay!' they cheered and dived in.

I shook my head at Trevor, got up and went into the boys' bedroom taking Ben's now vacant bed. 'Good luck getting them back to sleep,' I thought.

A few moments later Trevor poked his head in and said, 'Sam! Sam, come in the fun bedroom! Come on! Come and get in with Daddy!'

'How could you do that to me?' I thought, screwing my eyes up tight.

'No,' Sam grumbled into his pillow. 'I want to stay here.'

'Sod you then,' Trevor said and went back to the 'fun bedroom'.

I lay there listening to them giggle. I had flashbacks of me and my dad on those Saturday nights when he came home happily drunk and the magnetic bush had got him. How we laid in his bed and read storybooks and everything was perfect. My mum didn't get in my bed on those nights because she was pissed off with my dad, she did it because they had an agreed routine. My dad had his night out and then he would have some quality time with me. He looked forward to it as much as I did. He wasn't doing it to be spiteful to my mum. And that was how it dawned on me. That was the last straw. Everyone's relationships were not like mine. So I shouldn't just accept it as a fact of life. I had run a bloody marathon for God's sake. If I put my mind to it, I could do anything. If I put my mind to it, I could even get out of this bullshit marriage.

When he finally hauled his hungover arse out of bed the next day and came down sniffing around for some brekkie I told him, 'I'm leaving you.'

He squinted at me through bloodshot eyes. Then he said, 'Good. Go then.'

16

"MUMS TO MARATHONS, CLAIRE HOUSE CHILDREN'S HOSPICE AND ALL THAT SHIT"

I went to the One Stop Shop. I needed to find out if there was any help available from the government. I didn't like to ask. But these were desperate times.

I took my number and sat down, looking around the waiting room at all the other people. Everyone looked either angry, bored or sad. I wondered if I looked like that to them. I longed to be out running with my girls in M2Ms: laughing, energetic, happy.

After watching the big hand on the clock on the wall dodder painfully from one to six I was seen by a friendly looking woman. I told her my situation and I was gobsmacked about the array of help she said was available.

'And of course you've got your child benefit,' she smiled.

'Oh no,' I said, 'we don't get that. We didn't qualify.'

When Sam was born, you'll remember, Trevor had offered to sort out all the paperwork for the child benefit, but then his application was denied.

'Why?' asked the lady.

'My husband earned too much.'

'No, that's tax credits. You will have got your child benefit.'
The assistant pushed her glasses up her nose, tapped away at
her computer for a bit and then said, 'Yeah, here we are. Mr
Trevor Bolton has been claiming it for… eleven years.'

Sam was eleven now.

'Child benefit?' I squeaked.

She nodded.

'My children's benefits?'

'Yeah.'

I felt just like I had at Dee and Ollie's party – burning with
embarrassment and fury. The assistant must have thought I
was either thick or dodgy. I made some garbled excuse and
got out of there as fast as I could, raced home and waited for
Trevor to get in.

At first, I paced around the house like a caged animal
and then I saw my trainers by the back door. 'Thank you,'
I whispered to them and I did what I always did when my
head was about to explode. I went out running. I ran and
I ran out in the open, Chaka Khan blaring through my
headphones, no one around for miles, and I soon felt the
fuse on the cartoon bomb in my head fizzle out and the
strength filling my chest. It's times like these, bouncing
through the countryside the uplifting soundtrack in my
ears, that I feel like I'm in a pop video, but it's much better
than that because it's real, the feelings, the euphoria, and no
one is going to say, 'Cut!' and we don't have to do one little
bit over and over until it's right. It's all right, it's all perfect.
And when I get back, I'm ready to take on anything.

'You've been getting the child benefit all these years?' I
said when he finally sauntered in.

He didn't even flinch. 'Well, how do you think I paid for
all the holidays and presents?' he said sitting on the stairs

and taking off his boots as if we were talking about the weather.

'But you told me we didn't qualify. Why did you lie if you're so sure you should have it all?'

'Coz you know what you're like. You can't manage a piss-up in a brewery.'

'But I could have gone back to work. I could have contributed but you didn't let me coz it was always, "Fucked if I'm paying for three lots of childcare," with you, wasn't it.'

He had never given me any regular housekeeping money. I had to ask him for cash if I needed it and he made me feel like a scrounger for our whole marriage. He controlled the money, what we did with the money, what we did period.

I called his parents to see if they could talk any sense into him. See if they could help me try and resurrect this marriage. I had always got on well with them. Vic was a funny old bugger, but Trevor's mum Jenny and I used to talk a lot. After a family Sunday dinner, Vic, Trevor and his brother would sit there with red-wine moustaches debating politics. Jenny and I would be so bored we'd clear the table and have a good natter in the kitchen instead. It was over the washing-up that we would divulge all sorts of things to each other. When I first told her how Trevor was so horrible to me, she sighed, as if she expected it somehow.

'What is it?' I asked.

'Well,' she said, 'you have to understand, Trevor comes from a… traditional family. His dad worked all the hours God sent to provide for us, so he had to miss things the boys did when they were growing up, and when he came home knackered at the end of the day, he expected to be left in peace. He wasn't big on praise. He thought that would make them soft.'

That made a lot of sense. I was grateful to Jenny for those chats, so I thought she might be able to help stop my marriage from going down the pan now, but when she and Vic arrived to mediate between me and Trevor, it seemed blood was thicker than water after all. Jenny took her little boy's side, as did Vic.

Just like in Japan all those years before, I was shoving things into a suitcase again barely able to see what I was doing through my tears, but what was worse this time was it wasn't just me that I had to worry about, it was my three kids too. I had done everything I could to make sure they didn't come from a broken home, but it was on another run one day, my beloved meditation, that I had the clarity of mind to know that a broken home isn't necessarily one where the parents have split up, but it can be one where the unhappy parents stay together and in doing so break each other and the kids that have to witness the destruction. So, yes, I was running away again, if you like, but I knew well enough now how running could often be a force for good and right now this was an action that was going to save not only my life but more importantly to me, my kids'.

I managed to find a new place for us. I rented, it was too small, but it was near the kids' school and all their friends. It was dead shabby and it had no furniture. I had to furnish it with stuff from the Women's Refuge. We had to do without a fridge for a long while, but Wirral nights are cold enough to keep the milk on the windowsill for a day or two.

Trevor stayed in the house and very quickly – within a few weeks – shacked up with a woman called Trish. I did not begrudge him finding someone else, I was just shocked at how quickly he'd moved on after we split up. So on the way to drop off the kids at Trevor's for his week, I mentioned to them that Trish would probably be there.

'Oh yeah,' Sam went, as if it was old news, 'we went to Claremont Farm with her and Dad, didn't we, Ben.'

'When was that?' I said studying Sam's face as much as I could while trying to keep my eyes on the road too.

'Ages ago.'

'What do you mean ages?' I asked, trying to sound cool.

'I don't know. Months ago.'

I caught my breath, held in the gasp of humiliation my body wanted to fire out. I didn't want the kids to see me lose it.

When I parked outside Trevor's, the doors were all open and the kids flew into the house and left me standing on the doorstep. They couldn't wait to get in and see their cousins on Trevor's side who'd come over from Canada. Trevor was having a barbeque for them. The weather was perfect.

I waited for Trevor to pop his head out so I could say, 'I'll pick them up from school next Friday,' or whatever, just a little handover, as you do, but no one came. I looked into the house and saw Trevor's sister-in-law walk through to the garden with a glass of white wine in her hand. She didn't see me. No one did. I could hear lots of chatter and music coming from the back. It was just like it always used to be when family — Trevor's or mine — came round for a do. I could see it all, but no one could see me. I was outside of it all, not just literally on the doorstep. It was like I was dead or something and watching life go on from limbo. I waited for a moment longer. I was sure the kids were all right, no doubt playing with their cousins already, so I went back to the car and drove off. I only got a hundred yards or so, turned round the corner and had to stop the car. I couldn't see for the tears in my eyes. I sobbed and sobbed, as if I was grieving.

'Pull yourself together, Rach!' I said wiping my face with my fists. 'Do you want to be there instead of Trish? Go back to all that shit?'

Of course I didn't, but I *was* grieving – not for someone and not for that life in there with Trevor, but for a life that could have been.

'I've started the divorce proceedings,' he said when I went to pick the kids up.

'Not surprised. I'm sure Trish doesn't want to be shacked up with a married man much longer.' That's what I wanted to say, but I bit my tongue and instead I said politely, 'OK, right. Well, I don't suppose it matters who starts the ball rolling, as long as we get divorced, ey?'

Even though it was what I wanted too, it was still a slap round the face, the fact that it was happening so quickly.

'Well, just to let you know,' Trevor said sheepishly, 'I've got a solicitor and I had to give them a reason why I wanted the divorce, so I said "unreasonable behaviour".'

'Oh, OK,' I said, taken aback even more than I already was. Then a little laugh escaped my lips at how barmy the situation was and I said, 'That's what I would have said I was divorcing you for.' At least, I would have done if I could have afforded a solicitor. 'So,' I was burning with curiosity, and I told Trevor as much. 'What are you giving them as *my* unreasonable behaviour?'

His reply tattooed itself on to my brain forever. 'Because of Mums to Marathons, Claire House Children's Hospice and all that shit.'

Yes, ladies and gentlemen, Mums to Marathons, Claire House Children's Hospice and all that… shit, that was what he called unreasonable behaviour.

Trevor tried to control the divorce proceedings as much as he did our marriage. He kept telling me, 'This is the way it's done,' as if he was a bloody divorce lawyer, constantly trying to plant the figure in my head that he wanted to give me as a settlement even though I had put three times as much cash into the house when we were first setting up home there.

I was going to need my own solicitor, but I couldn't even afford proper furniture for our little house let alone lawyers' fees. So I went to see a solicitor who gave her first half hour free. In that half hour I explained my situation – as quickly as I could, before the meter started running – and when she'd heard my story, the solicitor said I would probably be entitled to legal aid to cover a solicitor's costs, but I would need a referral from a domestic abuse organisation.

'*Why would I go to a domestic abuse organisation?*' I thought to myself. Sure, Trevor was a pain in the arse, but he never hit me. I left the solicitor's feeling worse than when I went in.

Back at home, I hadn't even bothered to unpack most of our stuff. It was still in boxes all over the tiny house. The boxes served as furniture as we didn't have much.

I'd started going to food banks so we could eat. That really rubbed it in how desperate I was. It was humiliating. I thought about how I used to travel the world to exotic locations, dancing in lavish theatres, feathers and jewels draped off me, soaking up the applause of thousands of punters. And now I was wrapped in a tatty old coat, hood up against the cold and against my shame, rummaging on trestle tables for a box of pasta and a few tins of spaghetti hoops.

When I got home with my handouts one day, the phone rang. It was Trevor informing me he didn't have any money so he couldn't give me anything. Simple as that. No attempt to meet in the middle, to work something out, nothing, even though I knew when he said he didn't have any money he meant he didn't have any money that he wanted to give to me. Money that I needed to look after the kids when they were with me.

I hung up. I could feel that 'room full of bubble wrap' sensation filling my head again. I could feel myself plummeting to depths I hadn't even felt before. I looked around for a diazepam. Necked it. I wanted to just sleep, but my bed hadn't been put together yet, it was still leaning up against the wall in pieces. So I collapsed on the couch.

I must have been there for hours. I *know* I was there for hours in hindsight. I came round and saw Sam and Ben standing by me. Sam's lips were moving but I couldn't hear what he was saying. He told me later that he was saying, 'Are you dying, Mum? Are you dying?'

I tried to move, but couldn't. Apparently I'd told Ben to get on his bike, go to the corner shop and buy some ice cream. Sam shouted at him to do as he was told immediately, thinking ice cream would help his dying mum. I have no idea why I said that. I mean, we didn't even have a bloody fridge to keep ice cream in.

Clare, from M2Ms, called while Ben was out. I answered the phone to her, but again I have no recollection of doing this.

'I'm lost. I'm lost,' was all I kept saying apparently, over and over again.

She knew something was very wrong and legged it over. Sam let her in and she just sat with me for ages, talking to me, gently coaxing me out of this trance I was in.

'Fucking hell,' Clare smiled at me, 'I've done a bloody marathon, like, but I'm gasping for breath just running round to your house.'

I think I managed a smile back.

'Looks like we need to train more,' she winked.

But I didn't train at all anymore. I just went into myself. I kept making excuses to the girls why I couldn't run. Clare and our Lynne covered for me, but I just couldn't get myself out of bed half the time, let alone run five miles.

I didn't want to be with Trevor anymore, but, even though I knew it was the right thing to have left him, I was devastated that my marriage had failed. I kept spiralling down and down, spending more time sleeping, more time hiding away from the world.

Then one Sunday, my doorbell rang. I wasn't expecting anyone. I certainly hadn't ordered anything. Perhaps it was a Jehovah's Witness. I was preparing to tell them where to go as I opened the door. But there was no Jehovah's Witness there. Instead, there were forty women in bright orange Mums to Marathons T-shirts all doing squats in my little front yard. There was our Lynne, Clare, Keels, Lesley and so many others all shouting at me the way I used to shout at them:

'Come on! Move that arse! Give me twenty squats! Breathe! Let me hear yers!'

Forty women of all shapes, sizes and ages, but all equally beautiful. It was the most wonderful thing I had seen since Harriet was born. All my girls trying to motivate *me*.

'It's about time we returned the favour,' Clare smiled.

'Hurry up then,' Lesley squawked. 'Get your trackies on and get out here before my legs go numb. I can't keep this up all fucking day, can I.'

17

MELISSA

When she was three or maybe four years old my daughter Chloe dreamed, like many other little girls and boys do, of going to Disney World in Florida. And when she was three or maybe four years old I promised her that before she was eighteen I would take her. I'm sure many parents say 'one day' they'll take their kids to somewhere like that and perhaps they do and perhaps they don't. Trouble with me is, I don't do broken promises. When I promise something I mean it. But where the hell was I, working at KFC, going to find the money to take the family to Disney World?

When she was sixteen, Chloe reminded me, 'You've only got two years to keep your promise, Mum. You're not going to break your promise, are you?'

I spoke to my husband Carl. He wanted to see the family have this trip of a lifetime too. Like me, he thought we could pay the bills, we could buy a new bit of furniture, but the kids wouldn't treasure the memory of shelling out to British Gas or how comfy the sofa was for the rest of their lives. The slight spanner in the works was now we had five kids – three of them I'd had with Carl and the other two with my previous husband. So we both got on with working seven days a week, all hours to save enough money to take nine people to Florida for three weeks. No, my maths is fine thanks. Seven in our family, yes, but also Chloe insisted on taking her boyfriend with her – she couldn't cope for three weeks without him. And my eldest son, knowing Chloe would be busy canoodling with her boyfriend all the time, wanted someone to hang out with too and decided that should be his father, my ex. 'Not one of your mates?' I said hopefully. No, no one else would do apparently. I spoke to Carl.

'It's your call, babe,' he said. 'I'm not going to deprive him of time with his dad, or deprive his dad of time with him neither.'

Days before Chloe's eighteenth birthday we had finally scraped together enough money. I was totally shattered, but we were all on our way, as promised, to Disney World.

When I got back from this holiday of a lifetime, I wasn't rested, recharged, rejuvenated or whatever you might call it; I was even more bloody knackered than before I left. Taking five kids, one kid's boyfriend and an ex-husband on holiday was no holiday for me it turned out.

Over the years I'd have a couple of months here and there where I'd go a bit funny, not wanting to speak to anyone, feeling really down, but when I came back from Florida and was back behind the counter at KFC staring out in a trance at the high street and the buses going by in the rain, I thought how great it would be to be hit by one of those buses. Then I could get a couple of weeks in hospital. That would be a true holiday for me.

I told Carl what I was thinking.

'Babe,' he said, 'do you think you should get some help?'

'Help? What do you mean? Ask someone to push me under the bus?'

'No! You know what I mean.'

'No I don't.'

'I mean, you know... psychiatric help or whatever.'

'Oh, what good are you? I'm not mental. I just need a break.'

'No one's saying you're mental...'

'You just want me to be labelled a loony.'

'That's the last thing I want. I just want you to be happy. I don't want the children to see you crying all the time.'

'Then give me a divorce!' I shrieked.

'You what?' Carl was as shocked as I was at the words spewing out of my mouth.

'Give me a divorce! Then we would split custody of the kids and that would mean I'd get every other weekend off.'

Carl put his arms around me. 'I'm not giving you a divorce, babe. I love you. And I know you don't mean it. Let's get you to a doctor, ey? You might just need a few tablets again for a bit.'

I said I'd think about it, but started leafing through a magazine instead. Between the articles on celebrities' depressingly gorgeous homes and holidays that were nothing like mine, I saw an article on running and how it was good for your mental health. I lit up another fag. I told people I smoked between twenty and forty a day, which meant I smoked forty a day, if I could get my hands on them. Most of the guys I worked with in KFC were Romanian. When they went home, I'd get them to bring me tons of dead cheap ciggies back from Romania. So me and running weren't obvious friends. I turned the page to the gossip columns.

The next day I went to my Family Group. I'd been going there for a long time. It offered all sorts of free courses on things like parenting skills, which I really needed when I had my first two kids at such a young age. When I got to the group that day, they announced that the following afternoon Rachel Brown would be coming to take anyone who wanted to go on a mile run as part of their initiative to promote good mental health. As soon as it was announced I remembered that article in the magazine.

'It's sign,' I said to myself. 'Put me down for it,' I told the teacher.

I knew of Rachel Brown. She was the Forrest Gump of the Wirral with her Mums to Marathons thing. She often came into KFC. She always ordered a Zinger Burger with extra mayo and extra lettuce. She seemed nice, so I thought it couldn't hurt to try out running with her.

I turned up the next day for the run, fag in hand, looking like I'd just been dragged through Colonel Sanders' deep fat fryer.

Rachel's face! She could see she had her work cut out with me.

My lungs felt as if they were soaked in acid and my legs were all over the place by the time we'd finished, but with Rachel's encouragement I actually ran a mile.

'Now you've run one mile,' Rachel grinned at me, 'you can run another, and another, and another until you've run a marathon.'

And I believed her. I was so hyped up, full of adrenaline, or whatever it was. I felt like I could give it a bash right then and there.

I rushed home to tell Carl. 'I've run a mile. I've run a bloody mile.'

He was delighted for me. He was a fitness fanatic himself, but it was more than that – he could see a light coming from me that he hadn't seen in ages.

Then I went and found the kids. 'Guess what?'

'What?' they grunted their eyes glued to their screens.

'I've run a mile.'

'And?'

'And I'm going to run a marathon.'

They nearly spat out their milkshakes, 'Yeah whatever, Mum. You ran a mile. That's a bit different from twenty-six.'

'Well, you watch this space, this time next year I will have run the London Marathon.'

They looked up at me like I was loopy.

I went back regularly to the running group and within a couple of weeks I could feel the cloud, which had been hanging over my head for so long, lifting, just as the article in the magazine said it would.

Rachel and I would chat during the sessions. She told me about her life. And I told her all about my story, my cloud.

'You would never know, to look at you, that you'd been feeling like that,' she said.

'Oh, if I could run away somewhere,' I said, 'and disappear for a month or two, I'd be gone tomorrow.'

At home that night Rachel phoned me up. 'Pack your bags! We're going away for the weekend.'

'Ey?'

'You, me, our Lynne and a couple of the other M2Ms girls. We're going to run, have fun, get pissed, let our hair down.'

'Oh… I don't know,' I said, even though I was tingling at the thought of it – time away. I couldn't imagine it, even though I'd often dreamt of it. 'I need to speak to Carl.'

'Of course you should go,' he told me. 'That's a brilliant idea. Go and have a great time, all right? This Rachel, she's a bloody godsend by the sounds of it.'

Rachel had sorted out a caravan in Anglesey. We ran all sorts of scenic routes around the area, even up a mountain, which had me virtually crawling along the ground because I'm terrified of heights. But we had a ball. And I was fast becoming addicted to running. I was entering every event you could possibly enter. I was never going to be the fastest runner, I knew that, I was always going to be the tortoise not the hare, but I wanted to do better, I wanted to get fitter and that meant leaving the ciggies behind.

The London Marathon was approaching. I was all signed up with Rachel and some of the other girls from M2Ms. I couldn't believe I was actually going to do this. The kids couldn't either, mainly because Usain Bolt was running it too. They couldn't wait to tune in on the telly and look out for me. Me and Usain Bolt in the same actual race? It was mad. If I was the tortoise, he was definitely the hare, except it was unlikely he would have a nap halfway round and let me overtake him.

'You better beat Usain Bolt, Mum.'

'You call me on the last mile,' Carl said, 'I want to cross the finish line with you.'

But a few days before we were due to go down to London, Rachel called me at work. 'I'm really sorry to do this to you, Melissa, but I can't do it.'

'Do what?'

'I can't do the marathon.'

I thought she must be joking, 'What do you mean, you can't do it? You're ten times fitter than I am, of course you can.'

'It's not that.'

'Well, what is it then?'

The line went quiet.

'Rach? You can tell me, you know.'

'It's money. I can't afford the fare down, the hotel and everything. I just don't have it. Not unless the kids go without. I can't justify it.'

She told me how things had got so bad for her she'd been using food banks.

I couldn't imagine doing the marathon without her. I told her I'd cover her costs for the weekend. Anything to make sure she'd be with me for the race.

'No, no. I'm not taking money off you,' she insisted. 'You have to cover your own costs. You pay your subs for M2Ms. You've given me enough.'

When I got home I told Carl.

'I don't want to do it without her.'

'I don't want you to do it without her either,' he said. 'She looks after you. I know you'll be safe with her.'

Carl turned up on Rachel's doorstep. He handed her a few hundred quid he'd been saving for some fishing gear he wanted.

'What you've done for my Melissa... You've saved her life, literally. And what you've done for her has changed my life too. You've saved our family. So this is the least I can do. I won't take no for an answer. Please run with her on Sunday. She needs you.'

We had such a fab time in London. Seeing the sights, eating in nice places. Except for the night before, when Rachel insisted we had jacket potato, chicken, broccoli and baked beans. Good running food apparently, but broccoli and baked beans on the same plate? She also insisted we had a pint of Guinness each. It's good for you apparently, but it tastes disgusting.

'Doctors used to prescribe it for pregnant women back in the day,' Rachel said trying to persuade me to drink it all.

'Thank God they don't these days. Imagine how much I'd've had to drink with all my babies! Urgh!'

When I crossed the line with Carl and the kids on FaceTime I would have burst out crying if I'd had the energy, but Rachel cried enough for the both of us. I was so happy she was there and I could see she was too. I refused to take my medal off all night and the next morning I was skipping around the hotel room while Rachel groaned from beneath her duvet, happily knackered.

18

TOO MUCH WAFFLE MIX

Since the girls had turned up doing squats in my front yard, I threw myself into Mums to Marathons even more than ever. We already had the clubs in Bebington, Wallasey, Prenton and Morton and now I found myself setting up and leading clubs in Manchester, Heswall, Chester, and Ellesmere Port. It was my way of dealing with the trauma of this divorce, of course, but it was also a way to make a bit more money. I poured most of the girls' subs back into the club, for example buying the bright orange T-shirts and hoodies with the club name emblazoned on the back, which got us the name of the Orange Army locally. But I didn't feel bad about profiting a bit myself from it. It was my job after all. My only job. The only job I'd been *allowed* to have in years. And it was the best job ever.

I kept this all above board, of course, and got someone to do my books so I could declare my earnings. I wasn't keen on getting an accountant since the last one I'd had did a runner with all my fixtures and fittings from the Japanese restaurant, but there was no way I could do my own accounts – I might have my sights on giving Paula Radcliffe a run for her money, but Stephen Hawking was quite safe. So a friend introduced me to Mark Williams, who turned out to be brill – not only a great bookkeeper but an advocate too.

I was always on the lookout for new and exciting challenges for both myself and the M2Ms girls to try. I heard about the Anglesey Half Marathon when I'd gone on that girls' weekend with Melissa. It was billed as the most beautiful half marathon in the UK. It was supposed to have one of the most incredible start lines in the country: a completely closed road on Menai Suspension Bridge. Then it flowed downhill through Menai Bridge town centre and along the winding roads to Beaumaris. They said the route was flanked by breathtaking views of the Snowdonia National Park and the Menai Straits and finished in the centre of Menai Bridge town.

Plenty of the girls signed up. We'd go down on the Friday and make a weekend of it, running on the Sunday.

The Monday before that, I went for my annual mammogram. Just a check. Most women have them every three years, but I had to have them every year because I was deemed high risk: my mum had had breast cancer at fifty-two, but had luckily survived, an aunt had died of breast cancer, another aunt was stage four, so I never missed an appointment.

'Fuck me,' Lesley said when I told her I was going as we trained one night. 'As soon as I turned forty I needed to hire an assistant to book in all my bleeding medical tests.'

'Tell me about it,' I said. 'Do men have as many bits to test as us?'

'I'm sure they should, but I have to threaten to withhold all blow jobs from our Lee just to get him to see the GP.'

'I do these mammograms every year, but I'm always nervous beforehand, like.'

'I know,' Lesley squealed. 'They tell you not to wear any talc, deodorant or antiperspirants, but if there was ever a fucking day you needed antiperspirants, it's that day. As soon as they tell me to whip my bra off I stand there with my arms crossed under me tits, trying to defy gravity until the last possible moment, you know what I mean, like?'

I could barely run anymore for laughing. I knew exactly what she meant. 'And then you have to go and lay your boob on this giant... medical altar, like.'

'And some of us have more to offer than others,' Lesley said, sticking her big boobs in my face.

'But they're never satisfied with the way I lay my... offering on there. They always have to come and jiggle it about.'

'They're just copping a feel, that's all,' Lesley cackled. 'It's when that lid comes down and squashes your boob. Christ, mine looks like when I put too much waffle mix in me waffle maker.'

With Lesley's words tickling my ears I watched, the next morning, as that lid thing came down, hoping it would actually stop before it did more harm than good to my own waffle mix. Then the machine clanked and whirred away and, so quickly, after so much preparation, it was over.

'We need you to come back on Wednesday,' the doctor said.

'Why? What's wrong?'

'Nothing's wrong,' she reassured me. 'We've spotted a couple of small areas where the tissue is thicker than usual, but it's probably nothing. We can do a biopsy on each breast on Wednesday just to be sure.'

It wasn't funny anymore.

I went back on the Wednesday for the biopsies, which were hideously painful and I got a call the following day.

'You need to come back tomorrow to see us. Can you make it at eight o'clock in the morning? And please bring somebody with you.'

Well, of course, I just assumed the worst.

'No, don't worry,' said the receptionist, 'it's just they need to do a few more biopsies, just to be super sure.'

'I can't,' I said bluntly. 'I'm going to Anglesey tomorrow.'

Even though I was being told that they still couldn't rule out me having breast cancer, something which had killed or was killing members of my family, I couldn't let my M2Ms girls down – they were my family too.

'Well, it is very important.' The receptionist urged me to come in. 'We think it would be good if you could do this first. Then go on your trip to Anglesey by all means.'

Trip to Anglesey. She made it sound like a pathetic little jolly. She had no idea how huge this was for so many of us that were going.

The next day I went to the hospital at eight, as instructed, and I brought my cousin with me. Again, I had to go through those horrific procedures. I bled an awful lot and when it was done my boobs were bandaged up. I could barely walk let alone drive, so I could see why they'd asked me to bring someone along. My boobs were so sore there was no way I could run a few metres now let alone a half marathon with them bouncing around as they do, however good my sports bra was. Not that that stopped me going to Anglesey. Even if I couldn't run myself, I was going to be there to support my girls, especially the relative newbies, Ellie and her daughter Becky. It was their first big race.

19

ELLIE

It was 2007 when I made my first appointment with the doctor. It was totally out the blue for a lot of people but it was something I had been struggling with all my life. I had everything you could ever want. The house, a beautiful family, a good job. But I could never be truly happy; there was always something in the pit of my stomach gnawing away at me and it took me until my late thirties to start to come to terms with it. Things were becoming so bad that I knew if I didn't address this head-on it wasn't going to end well.

Four years of assessments and counselling followed that first appointment. There were times when I wondered if it was all worth it. It was often as traumatic as the struggle I'd been bottling up all those years before.

No matter how much anguish I was going through I'd always intended to hold on until my daughter Becky was sixteen and she was done with the main part of her education – she didn't need to deal with my problems when she was worrying about growing up too. But when I told her, she couldn't have been more supportive. My wife was as supportive as she possibly could be given her life was in tatters as well because of all this. But she had seen up close the turmoil I was going through and she knew as well as I did that it couldn't go on.

Supportive is a strange word to use in this situation really, because it's not as if it was a lifestyle choice for me. Transsexuals have no choice about what we are. You cannot ignore this condition. It will take your life, as it nearly took mine. It will become harder and harder to stay on this planet unless you get the treatment you need and soon.

So my wife and I divorced amicably in 2010 so at last I could begin living as my true self.

I began the hormone therapy. Within two months of taking them I saw the first changes on the back of my hands. The hairs that had sprouted there during puberty had fallen off. The skin was softer; those elephant wrinkles you get on your knuckles were smoothing out. Six months later and the stubble on my chin disappeared, helped by seemingly endless electrolysis. In fact my whole jaw seemed to change shape and soften as my flesh redistributed itself around my bones. I was mesmerised by my budding boobs and my hips, which looked wider, and my waist, which looked thinner. I felt like those vanilla candles you burn to make the room smell nice – a cold stick of wax, warming up, melting and malleable, quietly transforming into something softer.

It wasn't as simple as just popping pills though. Shedding the shell of Robert, who the world had told me I was since I was born near York in the seventies, was a harrowing journey, both emotionally and physically. It took me a long time to look in the mirror and see the real me: Ellie. I needed a lot of reconstructive surgery to my face, not to mention the gender realignment surgery. I had my final operation in 2013, but none of this could go ahead until two clinical psychologists had agreed that I was gender dysphoric – in other words, the woman I had always known myself to be.

I was tying myself up in knots with worry about what my colleagues would say when I went back to work as Ellie. I'd go through every permutation of every scenario in my head and it never went well. I had been in the same job for twenty years, where everyone knew me as Robert. I worked as an engineer for an airline – it couldn't have been a more masculine environment. But that worry turned out to be wasted energy. Everyone, at least to my face, was really good about it.

When I got my gender recognition certificate I could change my birth certificate too. Cradling in my hands that new formal declaration of who I was to the world – who I knew I always really was – was as monumental as cradling your first child, but the child was me, reborn.

In 2016 my workplace had a restructuring of its own and I got a new position in the company working as a supervisor with my colleague Kelly. We got along really well and we'd chat a lot when we got a minute to have a break.

'It's not like being an engineer. A lot of sitting on your bum all day here, isn't it,' I sighed.

'I know,' Kelly said. 'That's why I started going to this running club in Bebington.'

'Oh yeah?'

'Yeah. Mums to Marathons, they call it.'

She saw the look on my face.

'No, don't worry you don't have to do a marathon. Well, you can if you want to – it's amazing what some of these women do – but it's just great fun and the woman that runs it is brill. She's so friendly, so approachable. She'll get you doing stuff you didn't know you could.'

The look on my face wasn't really a reaction to the *Marathons* in Mums to Marathons – I'd loved running back in the day, and in the late eighties / early nineties I'd done a few half marathons myself. No, the look on my face was a reaction to the *Mums* in Mums to Marathons. Kelly explained that it wasn't all mums, any woman was welcome, but that was just it. It was a women's running club. It would be a big step for me to go to a club exclusively for women. Even though I'd been living as Ellie for a number of years now, it didn't stop that imposter syndrome bubbling up now and then.

'You should come too. It's great exercise and a great laugh.'

'Hmm,' I said, my voice about as non-committal as it could be. 'Might do.'

After a bit more persuading from Kelly, I found myself gathering with all these other women outside the library one Monday night at 7 p.m. Apparently they used to gather outside the school, but some of the neighbours had complained about the noise of fifty cackling women so they had to find another meeting point. I was a bit intimidated – they did make a racket, all these women, laughing and gossiping together. I was convinced they would sniff me out when I walked up to them and reject me as an outsider, not truly one of their own. But Rachel was on me like a shot. She took the beginners group and she made sure she ran with me at first. She was just as Kelly had described her. Warm, energetic and encouraging. And above all hilarious. I laughed so much on that first night. And I realised then I hadn't laughed, really laughed, for so many years. For as long as I could remember I was focused on the void in my life living as a man. And then the transition was a litany of trauma, emotional and physical. It was so good to laugh and be accepted in a group of women who never once asked prying questions. We were too busy having fun.

It wasn't long before Rachel was telling me her life story. I was quite surprised in fact about just how much detail she went into about the traumas she'd been through, as well as surprised at how she found the breath to talk at all as we ran farther and farther through the countryside. But her openness unlocked something in me and I quickly found myself wanting to tell her all about me too. The endorphins from all the exercise shifted me to a great mental state and I quickly found myself in a better place than I had been for a long time.

Less than a year after starting at the club Rachel told us we'd be doing the Anglesey Half Marathon. I didn't think I would be able to do it and nor did a lot of the girls, but Rachel had a habit of setting the bar high and somehow getting people over it. If we wanted to achieve it, she told us, we'd have to start training three or four times a week as the event drew nearer. But she impressed on us that it didn't matter how long it took us to do thirteen miles, the point was that we did it. She was all about your mental state when running. Get that right and you could achieve great distances. And in doing that she was teaching us, consciously or not, that if we got the mental state right in other aspects of our lives, we could achieve anything.

My daughter Becky was turning thirty, she'd had her first child and was feeling the need to get back into shape, so I suggested she train for the Anglesey Half with me. We had been close when she was little, but, as many kids do, she distanced herself from her parents as she went through her teenage years. I thought running together might be a good way to bring us closer, give us a common goal, especially after everything I had put her through with the transition.

I was happy to see she jumped at the chance to join Mums to Marathons. Even though she'd never been a runner before, she loved it as much as I did and made friends with lots of the women there. We were both gutted to hear Rachel was not well enough to run at Anglesey because of the biopsies she'd had, but at least she was coming to support. I didn't know whether I could make it without her screaming at me to *move my arse* as we set off.

The route was stunning, but it was hard going. I hadn't done anything like this for so many years and as the race went on it started to show. Becky was struggling too as we began the final mile. And then out of the mist came this vision: Rachel in her bright orange hoody, clutching both her boobs as she ran alongside us.

'Come on, Ellie! Come on Becks! You can do it. If I can do it, you can do it,' she bellowed at us.

I looked at Rachel, imagining the pain she must be in as she jogged beside us, for us. Her breasts were still so sore from the biopsies and yet she was determined to get us across that finish line. How could we let her down?

Becky and I dug deep. We breathed as Rachel had taught us, we focused like never before.

'NOW GO, GO, GO!' Rachel screamed and dropped away before the last few metres, giving me and Becky the moment I will never forget: crossing the finish line with my daughter hand in hand. The photograph I have of that moment is one of my most treasured possessions.

Becky and I couldn't wipe the grin off our faces for days. And Rachel was as high as we were, she was so proud of us. I still annoy Becky like any parent annoys their child, but I think we're closer now than ever before because of that very moment.

That night we had an Indian takeaway in the house we were all staying in. I came down from the shower when I could smell the spices, my hair still wet.

Rachel pulled up a chair for me. 'Sit down, love, and I'll blow-dry your hair.'

'It's OK,' I said.

'It's no trouble, I'd love to do it.'

I hesitated for just a split second, then I let her.

All us girls were sitting around chatting as the food was laid out and I caught Kelly's eye. She knew me well enough to know I'd have to be very comfortable with someone to let them do something as intimate as dry my hair. And I was. I was comfortable with them all, but especially Rachel, who'd enabled me to prove to myself that I could recover. Recover physically from the trauma of transition, as well as mentally. It was another huge step into the world of women that I had been barred from for so long by the gender dysphoria. As I looked around the room at all these women with such different stories – nurses, bank managers, artists, waitresses, cleaners, CEOs, the unemployed, mothers, daughters, widows, black, white, straight, gay, scousers and wools – a grin spread over my face. I thought about what a connector Rachel was. Connecting women not just from various geographical areas, but from any social background, on a level that changes you forever.

20

ON THE BONES OF MY ARSE

It was 9 a.m. I was at my mum's house. I'd stayed over the night before because the kids were with Trevor and our Lynne had said we should both go round and have a nice night in with Mum. We'd had a glass or two of wine to celebrate my all clear from the biopsies and I could have done with a bit more of a lie-in, but Lynne was up and at 'em by 8 a.m., encouraging me to get up too. We were sat at the kitchen table having coffee and chatting when the doorbell rang. My mum had just gone upstairs and so she called down for me to answer the door for her. I could see a figure in a bright orange top through the frosted glass of the front door. Then it was joined by loads more orange tops. It had to be the Orange Army, but I couldn't think what they were up to this time. I opened the door.

'Hello,' said a man holding a microphone. 'Hello, hello!'

The Orange Army screamed with delight as I recognised Dr Hilary Jones from the telly as the man with the mic.

I spotted a cameraman and hid behind the door, glaring at my mum and Lynne who were grinning, clearly in on the whole thing – that nice night in with Mum was just a way of making sure of where I was this morning.

Dr Hilary coaxed me out from behind the door. 'Rachel,' he said, putting his arm around me. He smelt as nice as I always imagined he did when I saw him on the Lorraine Kelly show on breakfast TV. Hang on! It's 9 a.m. Does this mean..? I'm not, am I?

'Rachel, you are live on national telly on *Lorraine.*'

'Oh my God,' I turned away. I didn't even have any make-up on.

Dr Hilary turned me back to face the nation saying, 'She said, "Oh my God". She didn't even swear.'

It was later when I watched the whole thing back that I saw one of the M2Ms girls telling Dr Hilary that I might well swear when he surprised me, at which I saw Lorraine say 'I hope not,' and try to laugh away her terror at the thought of all the complaints ITV would get if I turned the air blue at breakfast time.

Dr Hilary carried on, 'Lorraine and I and all this group and many others who couldn't be here would just like to say thank you so much. You've done so much for so many people. Turned so many people's lives around with your encouragement, motivation, getting these women and many, many more running and getting fit and healthy, not to mention the many tens of thousands of pounds you've helped raise for charity. And it's all down to you, Rachel.'

'Oh, I've done nothing,' I said, trying to sound modest, bubbling with pride and squirming with embarrassment all at the same time.

'Well, we think you have done a lot more than nothing, Rachel, and we want to not only say thank you but we've got some treats in store for you too, which we'll hear more about after the break, but for now, back to you in the studio, Lorraine.'

The camera was put down and a guy with a clipboard explained to me that after the ad break Lorraine – the queen of breakfast telly herself – would be talking to me down the line from London and I would be able to hear her in the earpiece he was wiggling into my ear. He pinned a tiny mic to my top and I was positioned in front of the camera with all my girls and Dr Hilary behind me – I could tell he was there because I could still smell him. I was so nervous and I grabbed our Lynne's hand tightly as I heard Lorraine's voice in my ear – it was so surreal.

'Before the break, Dr Hilary gave Rachel Brown the surprise of her life. Rachel has helped over five hundred women in her community and beyond to get running and put a smile back on their faces. Are you all right, love? Have you recovered now, Rachel?'

'Just about. Still shaking,' I heard myself say. Me chatting to Lorraine bloody Kelly!

'So many people wanted to say thanks to you, we were overwhelmed by people who wanted to say that, in fact. And what you do is absolutely inspirational, it's fantastic. Are you going to keep it up? Is it going to get bigger?'

'It's going to get huge,' I said. 'I have lots and lots of plans and ideas.'

'It's going global,' said Dr Hilary over my shoulder.

I lit up then. That sounded good to me. 'Yes, global. Everywhere should have a Mums to Marathons.'

The next thing I know I'm getting a call from Marks and Spencer. They were doing an advertising campaign for their bank called #makeaswitch and they wanted to do a TV advert starring little old me. I was dead nervous, but they treated us like royalty. They came up to the Wirral and we did some shots in my house and they filmed me running on the beach at West Kirby at sunset. And then the next day we were down in a studio in London and they had me doing all sorts of stuff in front of one of those huge green screens like they use to put in special effects on superhero films. I had to wear Marks and Spencer's clothes and I didn't like the way they did my make-up but you can't have everything, can you.

As the director said 'Action!' I thought about Karen and I dancing in school all those years ago and Mrs Bo-ho Burns shitting on my dreams of becoming an actor.

'Look at me now, Mrs Burns, you nobhead!' I thought.

I was a film star. I *was* the next Bette Midler after all – at least for a little while.

All this attention just drove me to work even harder on spreading the word about Mums to Marathons, but trying to do it all on my own in all those locations, running all those miles in all weathers, while still being a mum to three kids, meant eventually I pushed it too far.

I ended up in hospital with pneumonia.

A painful week later, when I got out of the ozzie, I knew something had to give. But I didn't know what or how. That was when one of the M2Ms girls, who was a doctor in Ellesmere Port where I had set up one of the clubs, came to me with an idea that could save me and M2Ms. She said she wanted to put me in touch with two women – the head of Cheshire mental health services and the head of mental health services for the entire north-west.

'Why?' I said, thinking, *Bloody hell, I'm not that mental that I need to see the chairman of the board, am I?*

'Because of what you do for women,' she replied, 'what you have done for yourself. You've really made a difference to women's mental health round here. Our mental health services could really benefit from knowing about this.'

'Well, I'm not sure about that,' I said.

'Just meet them, will you?'

I expected two stern-looking women in suits, but they were actually very friendly women, in normal clothes, both of which were bawling their eyes out by the time I'd finished telling my story.

'This could be huge,' one said.

'We'd love to make this an NHS service if we could.'

'Oh my God,' I said, picking my jaw up off the table. 'Really? How do we do that?'

'First, we need to do a pilot, get some funding, so we can spread the word.'

This could be the help I needed, I thought, to keep spreading the word about running without running myself into the ground anymore. And what's more, funding from the NHS wouldn't go amiss since I was still skint. They told me they had hundreds of patients with mental health issues who they would send a letter out to inviting them to a talk that I would give – slide show, the whole caboodle – in the community centre next door to their offices to tell them all about M2Ms.

The big night came. Our Lynne, Lesley and Clare were all there in their M2Ms T-shirts to support. We all beamed at each other, rubbing our hands together as if we were about to go on stage at Wembley or something. My slide show was ready to go, a hundred or so seats lined up in front of me.

But when the start time of seven o'clock came, only one seat was full.

'What the fuck, like?' Lesley said.

'They sent hundreds of letters out, didn't they?' Clare said.

'That's what they said,' I growled, going next door to the office where I'd met the mental health service bosses to check.

'Oh,' said the secretary finding a pile of our letters under a pile of papers. 'Is this them?'

They'd forgotten to send out the letters.

'Oh that proper boils my piss,' Lesley snapped.

'It's OK, it's OK, Les,' I said before she went off next door to kick some arse. 'There's one person here. And she might need some help. At least I can help her.'

So I chatted to this one girl. It wasn't quite the show I was planning, but she started running with us anyway. And at home that night I went back to Facey, where I'd posted all those years ago about the joy I'd found in running. It had had a powerful effect back then so I wondered if I could do something similar now to recruit girls for this NHS pilot.

The first night of the pilot in Ellesmere Port I stood outside the community centre on my tod.

7:01 p.m. 'They're coming. I know they'll come.'

7:03 p.m. 'Bloody hell where are they?'

7:05 p.m. 'Please come, please come. Please don't give up before you even start. Please, please, please. I know you can do this.'

7:06 p.m. 'Oh fuck it…'

'I'm not late am I?' It was her – the girl who I'd chatted with in the community centre.

And then there were two more. And another. And another. And before I knew it there were ten, including the two mental health service bosses, all looking at me expectantly.

'Deja bloody vu,' I said to myself, thinking back to that night in 2013, the first time I ever took some girls running.

'You what?' one of the girls said.

'Oh, nothing.' I cleared my throat. 'Right. Before we start, let's warm up a bit.'

Everyone seemed to enjoy the session and when it was over, I asked one of the health service bosses when I would get paid.

'Where did you get the idea you would be paid for this?' she said with a worried look on her face.

I could feel my face going scarlet with embarrassment. Hopefully it just looked hot from all the running. 'Oh… Well… erm… you know, the funding?'

'We don't have funding for this. It's just a trial.'

'But when we first met, you were like, this is going to be huge, this is going to be an NHS service, funding this, funding that.'

'Sorry Rachel, we can't pay you.'

I was livid. Not just because I wasn't getting paid for training these ten women and I was still living on the bones of my arse, but because there were dozens of women back in Bebington and elsewhere who *were* paying that I had had to let down tonight because I was here.

21

HARK! THE GUARDIAN ANGELS SING

For the next eight weeks I stuck with the pilot, because I'd made a commitment to the women who needed it, though I never saw a penny for it.

So now without any support from the health services I had to let some of the clubs go. I felt terrible, but I would have felt worse knowing the girls were not getting my full attention.

I've already mentioned how Mark, my accountant, was more than just an accountant. That's because he would forever be introducing me to people that he thought might be able to help Mums to Marathons expand. He introduced me to someone from the Wirral Chamber of Commerce who offered me free office space, should I ever need it – although that looked increasingly less likely as I was closing clubs not opening more. But that guy in turn introduced me to Sandra Kirkham, the CEO of Pacific Road, a charity in Birkenhead which is concerned with the preservation and protection of health and the relief of poverty and sickness in the area. He reckoned she'd love to hear about my work with M2Ms. He thought it would fit with what she was trying to do for vulnerable people in the north-west.

I almost didn't go to meet her. I was really struggling with my depression at the time. I felt I was in a hole. I felt I had let so many women down and I was letting my kids down by not being able to provide for them. Christmas was fast approaching – and if any time of year is likely to play havoc with your mental health it's Christmas. Not only haven't you seen the sun for months, which is depressing enough, but then you're bombarded left, right and centre with adverts and images telling you you should be buying enough food to feed a small developing country, enough toys to stock Hamleys, and sitting round a table overflowing with wine and creaking under the weight of a giant glistening turkey with your perfect happy family, when your reality is nothing like that and you'll have to get into debt, which you might never be able to pay off, just so your kids don't feel left out among all their friends, whose families seem to be that perfect fucking family in the adverts.

I dragged myself along to see Sandra anyway. I didn't want to let down Mark, who'd got the ball rolling for me in the first place. She listened as I told her all about Mums to Marathons and she asked me about my personal journey, so I ended up spewing out just about everything I've spewed out on these pages so far.

Sandra sat back in her chair when I finally shut my gob.

'Sorry,' I said, 'I don't half go on, don't I?'

'No, no. I could listen to you for hours,' she smiled warmly. 'And I know you could help hundreds and hundreds of people. Many of the people my charity tries to help. I *know* that you can do that. We have this networking event coming up. Lots of charitable organisations will send representatives and I think they would all love to hear the kind of thing you just told me. Would you be a guest speaker?'

'Me?' I said, my eyes bulging out of my head.

'Yes. You'd be great.'

'Well… I… I suppose I…'

'Great,' Sandra clapped her hands together. 'That's settled then.' She told me when and where to turn up and just as I was about to leave she added, 'But, Rachel, you can't help anyone if you're struggling yourself, you know.'

I felt the blood drain out of me.

'So,' she scribbled out something and handed it to me, 'take this!'

She was handing me a cheque for a thousand bloody pounds, and as soon as that dawned on me I pushed it away, 'Oh I can't take…'

'Get the kids something nice for Christmas.'

'But…'

'Consider it your fee for speaking then.'

I didn't know if it was appropriate to hug a CEO, but frankly I didn't give a shit right then and I threw my arms around her.

The night of the event came and I was dead nervous. It was in the Pacific Road Theatre where the charity was based. I would be standing on that great big stage in front of all these people sat on tables arranged all over the floor. I hadn't stood on a stage in front of so many people since the last time I danced in Asia. The tables weren't full of dolled-up tourists, fine wines and glittery decorations this time – it was more tea and cake and sensible shoes. But this time I wouldn't be up there on stage in the safety of a troupe, disguised in feathers and jewels, while the audience were dazzled with lights and music. This time it would just be me, on my own, no costume, no smoke and mirrors, no dance routine, just me standing there in the middle of that enormous theatre, telling my story.

Just like when I used to dance in the Pleasuredrome a lifetime ago, I couldn't do this speech if I was doing it like people are trained to do – flash cards and bullet points and rigorously rehearsed. I couldn't do all that fancy stuff in public speaking just like I could never do ballet or tap or anything that wasn't natural to me. If I was going to do this speech, I would have to approach it like I used to approach dance: nothing rigid, nothing practised a million times. I would just get up there, open my gob and see what came out.

Sandra knew this so she put me on last: 'Then you don't have to stick to a time limit,' she grinned.

I watched the five or six other people get up and speak before me like I used to watch those other girls do their bombershays and arabesques in the auditions. And then I got up, shaking, but I told myself: 'Just do what you do. Like when you did your *Flashdance* impression in front of those agents in Manchester.'

As soon as I sat down after the speech, there was a queue of people wanting to speak to me. One of them was a lady from a charity that had helped me during the darkest days of my divorce.

'My name's Sue and I'm the CEO of Involve Northwest,' she said shaking my hand.

I was just about to start thanking her for all her organisation had done for me, when she carried on:

'Do you want a job?'

I looked at her, looked at all these people queuing up behind her, looked up to the gods and winked at my dad, who I knew was sitting up there enjoying the show.

22

CLARE

When I was pregnant with my first child, I began having these visions. I was thinking, 'Am I going doolally here?' But they kept coming:

I am upstairs as a three-year-old and my dad comes up with this belt. The belt has an eagle's head on the buckle. He whacks me with it. I run to my bunk bed, holding on to the bed post as if it will save me somehow, like some ship's mast in a raging storm. It doesn't. A buckle that shape can't half do some damage. There's blood. It streaks my underwear and I hide in the toilet for ages when I see that. I can barely sit down the next day. The skin is on fire like it's sunburnt – that extreme sunburn when your mum has to put on calamine lotion.

The more these visions came, the more I started to wonder if they really were just visions:

I am unconscious in the bath. Someone pulls me out. I come round and see my dad slumped on the floor, blood oozing from both his wrists where he has slashed them with his razor blade.

I got hold of all my records from my childhood and they detailed how I was in nursery one day and, as we got changed for PE or whatever it was, the teachers noticed all these bruises on my back. They asked questions and found out that my dad had beaten me with a frying pan for doing a number two in my kecks. It turned out I was his punchbag.

When I was two years old my mum said she was going to the bingo. But she never came back. She ran off with another man. My dad idolised her, but he wasn't the most exciting of husbands – he would just sit there most of the time watching telly with his leg wagging. My dad was left with me and my older brother and sister. He couldn't cope, had a bit of a breakdown and that was when he probably started taking it out on me. Not my brother, not my sister, just me. Did I remind him of my mum? Was I the one child too many that made my mum abandon us all? Whatever the reason, those visions I'd had weren't visions, but memories; memories I'd blocked out.

To help him cope, in 1974 we moved from Runcorn on one side of the Mersey to Speke, a suburb of Liverpool right on the widest part of the river, near to my nan and grandad, his parents. He must have got married to someone else pretty quickly too because I remember this woman called Dot moved in with us. I fucking hated her. She used to make me eat garden peas. I still hate garden peas to this day. And she must have had loads of kids of her own because suddenly the house was filled with them. They were everywhere you looked, even in the attic. But even with Dot around my dad still couldn't cope. That's when the teachers found me covered in bruises and I was put into care. I didn't know that was why I was being taken away from my family. I thought that was just what happened when you got to my age.

Myrtle Street Children's Hospital became my home for a while. It was a big red-brick building in the centre of the city that looked more like a castle from the outside to me. I had a metal-framed bed with peeling paint, like all the other kids in the enormous ward who were in for some illness or another. When I first got there the doctor would come and draw the curtain around the kid next to me as he examined her. I kept letting my toys roll under the curtain as if by accident. Then I had an excuse to crawl under as if to get my toy back, when I really just wanted to have a nose, see what the doctor was doing to this kid. I got a bollocking of course.

After a little while I was moved to Heswall Hospital on the Wirral. It was more like a great big mansion house set in these big parklands, and the wards were just as big as those in Myrtle Street. I had my bed and my side unit and that was my world. Plus the creepy caretaker who used to stand there watching us as we got dressed, so we all used to try and hide behind our side units as we pulled on our clothes. Apart from him I quite enjoyed my time there. I loved the open space and the staff would take us through the grounds where there was a big old steam roller just sitting there that we could all play on before going down to Thurstaston village with its beach and heath.

When I was seven-ish I was moved to Abbot's Lea Children's Home in Liverpool city. We got a basic education at Abbot's Lea, but it was nothing Oxford or Cambridge had to worry about, if you know what I mean. My nan worked there as a cook. I don't think that was a coincidence. I think it was a way of beginning to integrate me back into the family because my dad and my two siblings were now living with her and my grandad. I used to help my nan in the kitchen at Abbot's Lea. It must have been 1981 because it was the year that Bucks Fizz won the Eurovision Song Contest with *Making Your Mind Up.* Everyone was talking about it, not so much because of the song but because of this dance routine they had where the lads whipped the girls' big skirts off to reveal tiny mini-skirts underneath. We used the tea towels in the kitchen to stand in for the big skirts which we'd rip off the waists of the girls playing Cheryl Baker and Jay Aston. I dreamed of being Cheryl, but I always had to be Mike or Bobby, doing the ripping – I was not girly enough apparently. Always a bit of a tomboy.

The year of Bucks Fizz was the year I started going home at the weekends to my nan's. The school would drop me off there in their Variety Club Sunshine minibus, which my brother and sister would always take the piss out of me for, saying I was a 'window licker'. But soon enough, at the age of nine, I was back full time, living with them and my grandparents as well as my dad, who had left dotty Dot for some reason. Me and my sister shared the smallest room. My bed was made from an old door. My dad and brother shared another bedroom. Dad left me alone pretty much – from then on I always looked on my nan and grandad as my parents.

I went to the local school, a proper school for the first time in my life. It was the last year of primary though, so friendships had already been cemented among the kids there and I was just this new random who turned up in big stacked shoes and tatty clothes. I knew they were taking the piss out of me so I played the clown to try and make them laugh and avoid getting picked on. But every so often I would get pulled out of lessons because I had to go and see a psychologist or a social worker. That did nothing to help me fit in, but I didn't really understand why I was being singled out for this attention from the shrinks.

I went through secondary school and found sport was my thing. I did hockey and athletics. I ran and threw javelin for the Liverpool Harriers, a renowned club which produced some international champions. In my early teens Liverpool Women's Hockey Team asked me to start training with them. I was made up. I told Nan, bouncing around the kitchen as if I was in Bucks Fizz again.

'Well, there's no way you're going all the way over there by yourself,' my nan said.

'Why not?' I asked, like someone had let all the air out of me.

'You'll have to get your dad to drive you. You can't go out on your own these days, not with that pervert hanging around.'

Some weirdo had started calling the house saying he'd been following me and my sister.

He'd say something like, 'You were wearing nice pink leg warmers today,' so we knew he'd been watching us.

'Nan,' I'd shout. 'It's the pervert again.'

I could only hear this heavy breathing down the phone now, so I handed it to my nan.

''Ere,' she'd say to him, 'you better get yourself to the doctor's. Sounds like you've got a sore throat.' And she'd hang up.

I could see from her face she was rattled, but she wasn't going to let him know it.

Then one day my sister was alone in the house and he turned up at the door. She opened it thinking it was my dad or grandad and he tried to force his way in. She fought him back and managed to close the door before calling the police, but there was no way my nan was going to let me go off to hockey training on my own after that.

So, when he got home from work at the Ford factory which was right opposite our house, I asked my dad to drive me. He huffed and puffed – it must have been that long commute he had.

'I'm not doing that,' he grumbled, 'God knows how many times a week, all the way over there.'

So that was the end of my hockey career. Just like that. And I never forgave him for it.

I decided on a career in the army instead.

'The army's full of dykes,' my nan said. 'You're not joining the bloody army.'

So that was the end of my army career. Just like that. I did forgive her though.

'You need to do a lady's job,' she said.

'All right then,' I said, 'I'm going to do hair and beauty at college.'

Nan seemed to like that idea. I bloody didn't. There was no way I was going to be a hairdresser or some dolly bird cosmetics assistant. No, I wanted to do special effects make-up, horror, blood and guts stuff in the movies. I'd called up Pinewood Studios to see if they could offer me any training, but they told me I'd have to go and do a basic hair and beauty course first – that was the only reason I was doing it, unbeknown to my nan, of course.

The college was in the Wirral, you could see it from our house in Speke across the Mersey. If I'd had a little rowing boat I could have got there in twenty minutes, but as it was I had to go all the way into town and then out again through the tunnel. It took well over an hour, so I thought, 'Sod that!' I got a job at the new McDonald's near college to pay my rent and moved in with a load of mates I'd made on my course. Nan made Dad give me a hundred quid to help me on my way. You should have seen the face on him. It nearly choked him handing over that, I can tell you. Short arms, long pockets, my dad.

I loved living on the Wirral. I always used to think it was dead posh compared to Liverpool. They had flowers and grass and everything. Most of my friends growing up came from the inner city, so that was what I was used to, the concrete jungle, the rough side of urban life.

My sister called me a plastic scouser when I moved across the water – and I suppose I am now. My accent has softened so much over the years being this side of the water. But it is just as much of a mishmash of rundown parts and Yuppified areas as Liverpool is when you get to know it.

So I was enjoying life in my late teens, except for this nightmare I always used to have:

I'm in this derelict building. I know it's my college, but it's just a burnt-out shell in my dream. And all these faceless people are trying to attack me. I jump out of a window to escape. They try to grab my legs, but just before they can I fly away. Free.

When I went to Portugal on a holiday with some workmates from Mackie's, the nightmare stopped. I knew it was my head telling me something. So I jibbed the course in, stayed in Portugal and began working in a restaurant in Albufeira. My boyfriend Dave followed me over. We had nowhere to live at first so we slept on the beach, keeping clean by using the beach showers, until we could afford a diddy apartment. We soon changed jobs and started working in a nightclub. We'd roll out of there at sunrise and stop at the bakery on the way home: the smell of bread fresh from the ovens was boss, the sound of the old dears sweeping their doorsteps was like music, and the two old fellas playing chess outside in the square looked like something from a movie. Life was sweet...

...until some local bloke pulled a syringe on us and threatened to stab us with it if we didn't hand over all our money.

Something snapped in me after that and I decided to go home to England. I called my nan for some help with the plane ticket. She made my dad pay for it.

'I will pay you back, Dad, don't you worry,' I told him. I wasn't going to let him have that hanging over me forever.

When Dave and I got back to England, I found out I was pregnant. And that's when the visions – or rather, the memories – started coming. It was traumatic enough giving birth for the first time let alone discovering all this stuff about my childhood, but it just made me determined to make sure my kid didn't have a childhood like mine.

Dave and I got a flat – it was full of damp and smelt funny, but it was our own. So I got on with giving it a lick of paint. I was ready to pop at this point but tried to put the wallpaper up myself too. It looked like a bar of Aero when I'd finished, there were so many bubbles trapped behind it.

Dave just watched.

I was twenty-one when I had our Daryl, my little Ginger Ninja. I was glued to the telly in the hospital even though I was bent double with contractions, because it was the night the house blew up on *Brookside*. I couldn't miss that, could I? I was off my head on diamorphine and pethidine – it was great. But now I was a mum I put a stop to any other drug taking. I'd done pot, the odd bit of speed and pills in the past, but not anymore. I had responsibilities now.

Dave didn't see it the same way.

I had three or four jobs: cleaning, bar work, that sort of thing, but Dave had nothing. He spent all his time getting stoned with his mates in our flat with our baby in the next room.

I started to realise he was no good for me, but I stayed with him because I was more determined than ever that our Daryl's childhood would not be like mine. Daryl was going to have a dad *and* a mum and he would be farmed out to some kids' home over my dead body.

When I had my second, Dean, my Mr Potato Head, I was sure that would be the wake-up call Dave needed, but nothing changed. And I still couldn't, wouldn't leave him. I would not have my kids feeling abandoned by either parent, like I did.

Soon Dave was gambling and even doing coke. I was actually repulsed to be near him and my mental health was starting to suffer so much that I knew if I didn't get out I would end up topping myself. Our debt was spiralling because as fast as I was earning money, he was gambling it away, so I started secretly saving, working even more jobs and extra hours so I could afford a place of my own with the kids. Even though I'd paid for the majority of the place I shared with Dave, I just walked away from it because my mental health was much more important than bricks and mortar.

I never stopped him from seeing the boys. There was no way I was going to do that after all I'd promised myself about protecting my kids from feeling abandoned, but knowing that, Dave refused to see them, refused to help them out, pushing my buttons to get back at me for leaving him.

I did meet someone else eventually: Neil. And we had my third son, Finlay Fat Head, together. Neil and I were together for sixteen years because in many ways we were compatible. I was obsessively clean and tidy – I wanted everything just so; I needed to control my home and the only person I trusted to look after me was me, which was not surprising when I had no one but myself to trust in for so many years growing up – and Neil was happy for me to take the reins; he allowed me to mother him, just like his own mother had done everything for him in the past.

'But what about you?' said one of my oldest mates, Sarah, when she came round and saw me up to my eyes in ironing, while cooking his tea before going out to work.

'What do you mean?' I said as if she was talking Portuguese, which I never got the hang of when I was there.

'What about doing something for you for a change?'

'Like what?'

'You used to love your sports. What about getting back into that?'

I remembered the buzz I used to get from running with the Liverpool Harriers, throwing the javelin and whacking a hockey ball around a field, but I just laughed it off. 'I can't even run up the stairs these days,' I said to Sarah.

'Tell me about it. But I'm far less fit than you. Is that really an excuse?'

Sarah was right. I had no good excuse. I shrugged.

'Then you need to get back into training,' she smiled.

And so I found myself running alongside this nutter called Rachel at some club called Mums\ to Marathons. I call her a nutter because within half an hour of meeting her she's spilling her guts out on the pavement in front of me. I was much more reserved. At least at first. But everything she told me – being the clown at school to try and make friends, feeling the odd one out, the psychosis and visions when pregnant, the shitty husbands – everything resonated. It was like we were twins. The more I heard, not just from Rachel but from other women in the group, the more I realised it wasn't just me that felt so let down and depressed. I wasn't weird because of what I had been through and what I was feeling. In fact it was all too common. My sense of isolation started to evaporate the day I joined the club. Having gone through what she'd gone through, Rachel should have had a wall like Berlin in the Cold War all around her, but she was such an open book. There I was, sitting behind all the walls I'd built up after a lifetime of disappointments and she was just exuding trust and was loved back in spades because of it. I really learnt from that. It was such a tonic. She made me believe in myself, believe I could make a change in my own life. It was like a therapy session on the street, no shrink's couch needed. I found a confidence and a clarity I hadn't felt in forever. And as I trained for the London Marathon, I had this feeling I could do anything if I could do that. So I did make a change. A big one. I realised I wanted to be a lover to Neil not his mother. I had three kids already thank you very much. I didn't need another. So I had a showdown with him. I told him to go away for a bit and think about what he really wanted, thinking he'd come back after a couple of weeks a new man.

He moved out for good.

Well, that wasn't the way it was supposed to go, was it?! What happened to this new invincible me?

I was devastated. I begged him to stay as I saw yet another family going to pot. I cried and I cried on my hands and knees as he packed his stuff...

...but the moment he left it was like a weight had been lifted from my shoulders and I realised that that was exactly the way it was supposed to go. That was exactly what the new invincible me needed and I had made it happen. I never looked back.

In 2016 I completed the London Marathon with Rachel and M2Ms. I smiled like a lunatic non-stop for the four hours and twenty minutes it took me to get round. I was invincible after all.

'Right, Rach, what's next?' I said as we pounded the streets one night not long after.

'How about the Berlin Marathon?'

'Berlin? Where they tore down the wall?'

Rachel nodded.

'Sounds good to me,' I beamed. 'Sounds bloody good to me.'

23

EVERYBODY WANTS TO RUN THE WORLD

With a new job in the bag I immediately began looking around for a new challenge – I know, perhaps I should've slowed down, just enjoyed being normal again for a minute – whatever normal is. But I can't sit still and that's my normal. I think I was slowly starting to realise that and embrace it, accommodate my mental health (or lack of it) instead of trying to run away from it.

'The Berlin Marathon? Sounds good to me.' Clare was dead keen when I told her my idea.

'Great!' I beamed. 'I'll start gathering the troops. We'll have to raise extra money this time and I want to do it for Claire House Hospice again…'

'Slow down, slow down!' Clare said. 'Us lot can sort ourselves out. You just concentrate on you for a change. Remember when you told me that? Well it did me the power of good. How about you run this one for you?'

I looked at Clare. I was so proud of how far she'd come. 'But you're coming, yeah?'

'Of course,' she grinned, 'I'm going for a new PB.'

*

Clare and I got to work, raising money and training. I asked Lynne if she was up for it.

'I don't think I'll be able to raise all that money this time, Rach. Not sure I'll have the time what with work and all that.'

I understood, of course, but I couldn't help being a little disappointed, until she said:

'I'm going to go up and do the Loch Ness Marathon instead. It's only a few quid to enter. It's on the same day as Berlin. We can run together but in different parts of the world. How about that?'

'Just you?' I said.

'Lew will take me up and be there for me, supporting, but yeah, you know I've always really loved Scotland and it'll be such a nice run to do, through the Highlands and all that.'

I hugged her. 'Look at you! Going off and doing your own marathons now.'

'I know! Who would have thought it, ey?'

I was as proud of our Lynne as I was of Clare.

Berlin is one of the big ones along with London and New York. Clare and I couldn't wait. It happens in September every year so we had all summer to train, but when August came I had to go into hospital for an operation.

For many years I'd had a condition called hidradenitis suppurativa, also known as acne inversa, which is thankfully less of a mouthful. It's a long-term skin condition where you get inflamed and swollen lumps, which are painful and break open. Women are three times more likely to get it than men – cheers, God! The areas most commonly affected are the underarms, under the breasts, and in me, my groin. Just what you need when you're a dancer doing the cancan in a leotard, ey? And then I became a long-distance runner, rubbing my thighs together for four hours at a time – some would say I was a glutton for punishment. But it was just one of those things – one of those many things – that I had to cope with and not let it rule my life or stop me from doing the things I loved. There is no known cure, so every so often I would have to go and have these gross lumps surgically removed from my groin, which is what I had to do that summer of 2017.

After the surgery they pack the wound with gauze and send you on your way while it heals. But it seemed to be taking a long while to heal this time, and I shouldn't have really trained for or run the Berlin Marathon, but I didn't want to let Clare down. And it was on my bucket list too.

So when September came, we flew to Germany and stayed with my cousin Mike, who lived in the city. We landed quite late on the Friday night (the marathon was on the Sunday), so by the time we got to Mike's it was 11 p.m.

We were in a nightclub by 11:30 p.m.

The next day we dragged our hangovers around the city by bicycle sightseeing and I wondered if we'd still have any energy to race the next day. After all that cycling I was also conscious of my groin which was still struggling to recover from the operation, but I was determined to run.

Sunday came and so did a flare-up of my diverticulitis. Oh yeah, didn't I mention I had that too? Diverticulitis, hidradenitis – you name an -itis, I've got it! While we're having a biology lesson, if you didn't know – and I hope you don't, unless you're a doctor, in which case, you should – diverticulitis is when small, bulging pouches form in the lining of your digestive system, most often in the lower part (the colon), and one or more of the pouches become inflamed or infected. It can cause severe abdominal pain, fever, nausea and a change in your bowel habits – which in my case was the squits every half hour.

'Are you sure you're going to be all right?' Clare said, looking anxiously at me as we found a place in the sea of runners at the Brandenburg Gate, where the race would both start and finish.

'Yeah,' I smiled, 'but there's no way I'm going to keep up with you. You go! Get that personal best! Don't worry about me!'

Clare studied my face a bit more, then gave me a kiss. 'All right. See you at the finish line. Love you.'

'Love you,' I said feeling energised by the fact that M2Ms had brought such beautiful friends into my life like Clare.

Then my phone rang. It was Lynne. She was on the start line at Loch Ness.'

'Ey, our Lynne. How are you?'

'It's blowing a bloomin' gale here. I'm freezing. Wearing a plastic bag against the rain. It's chucking it down…' she shouted down the line.

'Oh no.'

'…and I'm loving it.'

That energised me even more.

'Have you spotted Nessie yet?' I laughed.

'Not yet, but the route is next to the loch for the whole way virtually, so you never know. It's going to be hilly. The first six miles look to be all downhill. But it's blooming stunning, Rach. Wish you could see it.'

'You'll tell me all about it. That'll be as good as seeing it for me.'

I was made up to hear from her. She sounded like she was in her element and I was so pleased that, no matter where we were, we would always be connected by the magical medicine we'd found in running.

And then we were off. It was just as amazing as that first London Marathon I did. In some ways it was more special in that running was taking me to wonderful foreign places, just as dancing had once done. The crowd were fantastic and it didn't matter where you came from; it didn't matter that I was from the big bad UK which had just voted to split with the rest of Europe; today we were all one. Even the fact that my groin was sore and I ran like I'd been riding a horse for a hundred miles. Even the fact that I had to keep diving into a Portaloo every mile for a poo unless I wanted to do a Paula Radcliffe and shit on the road, though I didn't think I'd pull it off as coolly as she did in the London Marathon of 2005 – besides she only did it once; there would have been a twenty-six-mile trail of diarrhoea around the city had I tried what she did and that would have done nothing for our dodgy relationship with Europe. Even though it was one of the most uncomfortable marathons I'd ever run – and I'd run several by this point – it was still ace, not least because, when I came in an hour after her, I found out Clare had smashed her personal best. Mike was at the finish line and told me the air had turned blue as Clare had come in. She had torn some ligaments around her ankle about four miles from the finish, but she was determined to get herself over the line in a good time. And she did, in under four hours. We were both in a right old state with our various ailments and injuries, but we were as high as kites – no prescription needed.

24

HELEN

'You will probably have to use a wheelchair within a few years,' said the consultant.

I was forty-seven. For someone who was a gymnast and a cross-country runner in my school days, this was unthinkable. In fact I'm sure for anyone of that age it would be unthinkable. But in many ways it was not surprising.

When I was thirty, I was about to begin voluntary work as a mentor for social services. I had to have my photo taken for the council ID badge. As you do, I examined the photos hoping they were flattering and that's when I noticed one of my eyes drooping quite significantly. I mentioned it to my daughter Sara when I got home.

'Yes, I've noticed that before,' she said, 'but I thought it was just a bit of a lazy eye.'

I thought I'd better go to the optician to check it out anyway, and it wasn't long before I'd been referred to the eye hospital and then the neurology department and diagnosed with myasthenia gravis.

Myasthenia gravis is a very rare muscular disorder that's usually caused by an autoimmune problem, i.e. when your immune system mistakenly attacks healthy tissue in your body. In myasthenia gravis, antibodies, which are proteins that normally attack foreign, harmful substances in the body, attack the neuromuscular junction. Damage to the neuromuscular membrane reduces the effect of the neurotransmitters crucial for communication between nerve cells and muscles. This results in muscle weakness: the muscles of your face (hence my drooping eyelid), muscles we use to move about, muscles for swallowing and muscles we use to breathe. So, at any time, my diaphragm could decide to stop working and I would stop breathing.

I was at work a few months after the diagnosis and found I had trouble swallowing. I was rushed to hospital and underwent a thymectomy – removal of the thymus, which is a small gland that lies in the front part of the chest, beneath the breastbone, and extends into the lower part of the neck. People with myasthenia gravis often find their thymus develops tumours or swellings. I needed surgery to remove a tumour which was causing the issues with swallowing. Still I have to be increasingly careful about eating popcorn, nuts and things like that as the disease gets progressively worse and the throat muscles become weaker and weaker.

The exact cause of myasthenia gravis is unclear and there is no cure. It affects women at a much younger age than men. And because it's an autoimmune condition I am prone to many other problems. I regularly have to have surgery to remove other tumours – luckily none have been malignant so far – and I soon developed other immune system disorders such as rheumatoid arthritis, where the joints become inflamed and painful.

Three times as many women as men get rheumatoid arthritis; they tend to be younger when they get it and their pain seems to be objectively worse. I also developed Grave's disease, which causes overproduction of thyroid hormones and in my case that particularly affects the tissue behind my eyes, causing them to bulge and making them sensitive to light. Grave's disease is more common in women too. Yes, someone up there really seems to have it in for women.

The rheumatoid arthritis meant that stairs soon became difficult for me and my husband and I began making arrangements to move to a bungalow. But before we did, in early 2019, we went to visit my daughter in Dubai, where she teaches. I spent the entire time of what should have been a nice holiday in enormous pain, particularly in my back, and I found it really difficult to walk. So when we got back to England I went to see my consultant. He diagnosed osteoarthritis to add to my list of conditions. And that's when he said:

'You will probably have to use a wheelchair within a few years.'

'Is there any way to avoid that?' I said trying to sound composed, but feeling far from it.

'Well, the osteoarthritis is not curable. It will get progressively worse unless you do some kind of exercise to strengthen the muscles.'

The doctor didn't really go into any greater detail about what exercise to do or how I should do it.

Still in great pain and struggling to walk, I left the hospital and bought a walking stick, thinking my life was over at forty-seven. I had always been quite optimistic, despite all my ailments, but then I hit rock bottom. I had had enough. I had to take six months off from my job and my confidence was at an all-time low, especially when I was also diagnosed with autoimmune pancreatitis. I mean, how many more conditions could one person take?

I told Clare, one of my oldest and best friends, what the doctor had said about exercise. 'I've tried yoga, Pilates, nothing seems to do any good.'

'Then I think you should come running with Mums to Marathons,' she said.

'Running? Marathons?' I sighed. 'I'm not sure that's what the doctor had in mind. It's agony to get up the stairs, let alone run anywhere.'

'Trust me,' Clare said with a great air of authority, 'it's a different set of joints that take the pressure during running. I think it might be worth a try. And we'll all support you every step of the way.'

I had known Clare for about twenty years. She would call me every day to check up on me. I did trust her implicitly, so I thought I should give it a go. I had nothing to lose. And in August of 2019 I joined the club.

The training I got from Rachel, Lynne and Clare was second to none. They really knew their stuff. Rachel had her own array of physical problems to deal with, not to mention the mental ones, which inspired me to try harder to overcome mine. She pushed me in all the right ways, while respecting my limitations. And if I was at the back, which let's face it I usually was, she or Clare would be there with me supporting me every step of the way, just as Clare had promised. Don't get me wrong, it was hard at first, but Rachel instilled in me techniques which soon had more benefits than anything any doctor had ever told me.

I never used that walking stick.

I had been taking twenty-seven tablets a day including codeine, a powerful opiate painkiller, which can be addictive.

After joining M2Ms I was down to just sixteen tablets a day and nothing stronger than paracetamol for pain control. As I got fitter, my muscles strengthened and now, back at work, when I had the option of a lift or taking the stairs, I took the stairs – it was a good challenge. Meeting new challenges was something that M2Ms had made me ravenous for. And the sheer support and encouragement of this family of ladies makes you feel like anything is possible.

That's why in November 2019, just three months after joining the club, I was lining up at the start line of the Conwy Half Marathon in Wales.

The route sounds like a lovely picturesque stroll when the organisers describe it as passing:

> ...along the road adjacent to the Conwy River, proceeding towards Deganwy beach and the West Shore beach at Llandudno, from where it goes towards Llandudno Pier, then around the Great Orme taking in views of the Isle of Anglesey, Puffin Island and the surrounding North Wales coastline, before finally coming back to the seven-hundred-year-old Conwy Castle for the finish line.

But what they fail to mention is the Great Orme is basically a great big mountain and you spend half the event running up it and half running down it. It could be brutal at the best of times, but we were running in November on the tip of North Wales with the freezing weather lashing in off the grey Irish Sea – those views the organisers bragged about dissolved in the mist.

I almost had second thoughts. Rachel was there supporting and other M2Ms ladies were running, but I would have felt better about it if Clare had been there. Unfortunately she had some family do or something that weekend, which had been planned months in advance, and there was no way she could get out of it. She was always like the angel on my shoulder before M2Ms and throughout my journey with them, so for her not to be there now was a bit unsettling to say the least. Two months earlier I had done a local 10K. I couldn't believe I'd done that, but I'd had my twenty-one-year-old son Cameron, my greatest advocate, running with me then to make sure I survived it. This time I was on my own.

Rachel was there telling me I was going to smash it, as ever, telling me I was going to be fine, but as I queued up for the toilet beforehand I prayed, for once, the queue would never get smaller and I would miss the start of the race – that would surely be a good enough excuse to sit it out.

But the queue went down far too fast for a ladies' toilet.

I received my runner's bib and looked at it like it was an invitation to tea with the Queen – this can't be right. Why would I be putting on a half marathon bib when I was buying a walking stick a few months ago? But it was my bib, with my name and number on it. How could I back out now? I could blame one of my many ailments, I suppose – Christ, there was enough to choose from.

'All right, Helen?'

I recognised the voice behind me instantly. But it couldn't be. She was away at some family do. I turned round slowly and saw Clare standing there resplendent in all her running gear and with her race bib in her hand too.

'Oh my God,' I said, agog. 'Are you a sight for sore eyes. But what are you doing here?'

'I'm running. I've come to run with you.'

All the M2Ms girls around us giggled. They didn't seem surprised that Clare was here.

'You were coming all along, weren't you?' I said, trying to be angry with Clare, but failing miserably.

'I just wanted to see your face,' she smirked.

I gave her a good slap, but an even bigger hug. I'd always wanted Clare there beside me, but when she turned up like that at the eleventh hour it was even more wonderful, an even greater shot in the arm, such an emotional moment that gave me greater fuel to get over the Great Orme, and I'm sure she knew that.

Some of the girls had said they would run with me, but I'd told them it was OK – I didn't want to hold anyone back. If you're a faster runner, it can actually do you more harm than good to run at a slower person's pace, but Clare was there, she told me, to run with me, by my side throughout. She was one of the fastest runners in M2Ms, but she was prepared to sacrifice her needs for mine, which really sums up what Mums to Marathons is to the ladies involved.

Going down the mountain was more punishing on my joints than going up it, but Clare was there to rein me in whenever the pace got too much. She was that angel, literally over my shoulder this time – just what I needed to get me over the finish line.

I called up my family in floods of tears. Tears of joy. We all had a good cry down the phone at each other. In fact, it was a good hour after finishing the race before I stopped crying.

And then, just a few months after my triumph at the Conwy Half Marathon, coronavirus brought the world to a standstill.

With all my conditions I was highly vulnerable where COVID-19 was concerned, so going out running was not an option. But if I could keep myasthenia gravis, rheumatoid arthritis, osteoarthritis, autoimmune pancreatitis and Grave's disease at bay, there was no way I was going to let this coronavirus stop me either. So I bought a treadmill and did five miles every day from the safety of my living room.

After Conwy I was inundated with messages on Facebook from people, men and women, with various health issues, describing me as an inspiration. I was so proud to be able to give a glimmer of hope to them, just as Rachel and Clare had done for me and countless other people.

From my team of seven at work, now four of them run after seeing what it has done for me. And so the message spreads – that's the kind of virus we need to be spreading.

25

WISH IT WAS THE SEVENTIES AGAIN?

I had barely recovered from Berlin when I signed up for a charity cycle tour from Vietnam to Cambodia. Again it would be for Claire House Children's Hospice, which M2Ms had raised nearly half a million pounds for so far. Clare signed up too, as did another regular M2Ms girl Suzanne, and Katherine, the sixty-four-year-old who had, according to her husband, got her sparkle back by running with M2Ms and who was now unstoppable. If there was a mountain to climb or a jungle to trek Katherine was doing it. She had no intention of slowing down in her senior years. She was an example to us all.

Since we'd be doing sixty to eighty kilometres a day on the tour it would be wise for us to do a bit of training before we went. Katherine, Suzanne and Clare had bikes already to train on. I didn't. A good one seemed far too expensive, so I had to settle for a second-hand one from a charity. It looked OK, but on the first ride out I just couldn't keep up with the others. Now, I don't want to blow my own trumpet, but I was the one the others usually had to keep up with on foot, I was the one who'd clocked up the most marathons, so why, as they cruised along the river Dee towpath one hand on the handlebars chatting away, was I huffing and puffing, head down, face like a slapped arse, both in colour and expression? I soon worked out that the gears were buggered and so even on flat ground I was effectively doing resistance training. 'Sod that!' I thought, and I didn't go out again. It didn't matter, I told myself, one way or another I was going to complete the tour. I wouldn't miss it for the world. My will alone would get me through it – as well as a nice gel seat to ease the inevitable sore bum.

One week before we were due to fly, Katherine's mum passed away. Since Katherine was in her early sixties, her mum was a ripe old age and it wasn't totally unexpected, but nevertheless Katherine was obviously distraught.

'Don't worry about the tour, love,' I told her. 'These are special circumstances. I'm sure we can get your money back and sort everything out for you.'

'What for, Rachel?' Katherine smiled. 'My mum was dead proud of all the things I've done since joining M2Ms. And she would hate for me to miss this tour. I'm still coming.'

After the funeral, we flew overnight to Ho Chi Minh City.

'I thought we were going to Saigon. I don't see it on the itinerary,' I tutted.

'Oh you're so ditsy sometimes, you,' Clare said trying to get comfortable in the cramped seats for the fifteen-hour flight.

'What?'

'Ho Chi Minh and Saigon are the same place.'

'Really?'

She nodded with a smirk.

'Know it all,' I grinned, jamming my elbow in her ribs before settling back in my seat, happy in the knowledge that we were on our way to the sultry setting for that romantic and passionate musical *Miss Saigon*.

There was nothing romantic or passionate about Ho Chi Minh. It was a dirty, noisy, traffic-choked assault on the senses. Forty years ago, no one rode anything but pushbikes around the city, our guides told us.

'Take us back to the seventies then!' I said to Clare as we stood outside the hotel trying to take it all in.

'I've never seen so many mopeds in my life,' Clare said her mouth gaping until she got a lungful of diesel fumes then had to shut it tight.

We were both looking longingly at the Starbucks over the other side of the road, which called out to us like an oasis in the Sahara – well, not when we went to the Sahara because it pissed down with rain most of the time, but you know what I mean. It shimmered like a mirage in the heat haze coming from a thousand hot exhaust pipes. And, like a mirage, we thought we could never actually reach the shop and smell the coffee because there was a dual carriageway of insane drivers to negotiate first and not a pedestrian crossing in sight. We soon learnt there was no such thing as giving way in this country. It was survival of the shittest on the roads.

'Well, if these legs have taken us this far, I'm sure they can nip across there,' I said to Clare with a can-do voice but a face that might well have been looking at shark-infested waters.

'Run for it?' she grinned.

'LEG IT!'

We made it across alive for our fix of caffeine and watched from the safety of the Starbucks as entire families whizzed past on one little moped – Dad, Mum, three kids and not a helmet between them.

'Tomorrow we have to cycle through this,' Clare said, peering over the edge of her latte.

And after breakfast the next day, we did. I think I might have cycled through most of the city with my eyes closed, praying for no one to hit me but expecting a crash at any second. When we came to a roundabout, polite Englishness and giving way from the right would get you nowhere. In fact, it would probably get you killed. It was a free-for-all, which somehow didn't end in carnage. T-junctions were just as chaotic so the guide at the front of our group would just park his bike in the middle of the road to stop the traffic as we all wobbled through the junction out onto the next road.

We had a sixty-kilometre cycle that day to another city called Tra Vinh on the Mekong Delta. The weather was hot and humid so we stopped plenty of times for breaks and water. There were about thirty in the group and several were older – sixty plus – but they weren't as turbo charged as our Katherine, so it took a lot longer than the guides had anticipated to get to Tra Vinh and we arrived long after dark. That would have been fine except the bikes we were supplied with weren't exactly top notch. They were mountain bikes that had seen better days – those days when they were the only vehicles in Ho Chi Minh by the looks of them – and lights were far too fancy for these dream machines. So not only did we have to negotiate the streets of another bonkers city before we could collapse into our beds, we had to do it without being seen or being able to see the various obstacles all over the roads.

Day Two was a whopping ninety-kilometre ride to Can Tho through much more rural parts of the country, which meant less traffic but plenty of punctures on the roads that were basically dirt tracks. As we passed the shanty towns, rows upon rows of tin houses, the streets would be lined with little half-dressed children, all wanting to greet us.

'High-five! High-five!' they'd scream, our hearts would melt and we'd try and give them what they wanted while trying not to crash as we steered through the potholes with one hand.

By the end of the tour, kids would still line the streets whenever they heard we were coming through and try and 'give us some skin.'

'High-five! High-five!' they'd scream.

Our hearts would be as cold as ice now. 'Fuck off,' we'd mutter as we'd try to get past quickly, as quickly as our cramping legs and sore arses would let us.

Day Three was seventy-five kilometres to Chau Doc which was on the border with Cambodia and the following day we could relax a little as an enormous raft took us and our bikes downriver towards the capital of Cambodia, Phnom Penh.

'Optional tour to the Killing Fields,' Clare read from the itinerary. 'You going?'

'*The Killing Fields*?' I said. 'Wasn't that a film?'

It was, as we found out, far more than a film. It was a very real genocide in the late seventies when well over a million people were slaughtered by the Khmer Rouge communist regime.

'Still wish it was the seventies here again?' Clare said, squeezing my hand as we stepped through a wasteland where scraps of clothing stuck up through the soil like a strange, awful crop and we spotted teeth strewn about like terrible seeds. When we saw the memorial stacked from floor to ceiling with the skulls of those recovered from the mass graves, I thought about what I was doing when these people were being tortured and murdered. When a child's normal was having herself and her parents snatched away and taken to S-21, the school turned concentration camp where they endured unspeakable horrors to make them confess to crimes they might not have committed, my biggest concerns in Beb Sec were whether Mrs Bo-ho Burns was going to overlook me for yet another dance show and whether I was going to have to kick Jenny in the twinkle again for taking the mick out of my stammer. Running was definitely our medicine, M2Ms was our support group, but there's nothing like a genocide in a developing country to put our Western problems into perspective.

We left Phnom Penh the next day still reeling from what we had learnt and turned some of the anger we felt into energy to carry us through the next eighty kilometres to the city of Kampong Thom. From there, the next day, we cycled another sixty kilometres and lost some of the group as they started vomiting and feeling the effects of the intense heat and fatigue as we cycled. Luckily there was a bus on hand to pick them up and when we reached the next city of Siem Reap, it was the final destination anyway. We had a free day to explore the incredible site of Angkor Wat, hundreds of ancient temples some of which were being swallowed up by the awesome roots of humungous trees which had grown on and around some of the structures. It was truly out of this world. Like something from an Indiana Jones movie. And what made it more special was the thought that if I hadn't have shoved on my baggy joggers and hauled myself across town that night to that Zumba class all those years ago, if I hadn't have taken that first sweaty step towards getting back control of my life, I would have never been here, on top of the world, sitting with my sisters watching another stunning sunset over the magical temple tops of a wondrously spiritual place.

'Right,' said Katherine, wiping the tears from her eyes as the sun melted into the horizon. 'Let's go and get pissed.'

'Seriously?' I squawked. 'I'm ready for my bed.'

'Oh, don't be a bore! Just come for one then.'

'Shall we?' I said to Clare.

'Just one,' she sighed.

God knows how many later, we were all sat on the floor of a nightclub in Siem Reap's central strip doing the *Oops Upside Your Head* rowing dance, as locals and tourists alike looked at us just as we had first looked at the sea of mopeds a week ago in Vietnam. Then we were up dancing around the club and I was going toe to toe with a young black guy, copying every move he made, until I spotted a half-naked long-haired blond guy busting some moves on one of the podiums dotted around the room.

'Go on, Rach!' Clare prodded me. 'You could show him a thing or two.'

'Don't be daft!' I blushed.

And then he held out his hand to help me up to the podium.

He was a good dancer and I think he was surprised to see I wasn't half bad either. I felt like I was back at the Pleasuredrome in Birkenhead when I was free as a bird, with that same level of self-esteem that I had back then, which was given a further boost when the guy I was dancing with said in a German accent, 'I am interested.'

'Oh. Interested in what?' I said thinking he was about to tell me about his hobbies.

'Interested in you,' he said pulling me close. 'Do you want to come upstairs?'

I caught my breath, giggled to myself and then, after scanning the room for Clare, who was back by the bar, I said, 'Look, you're lovely and that, but I'm old enough to be your mum.'

That didn't seem to faze him, so I added, 'I've had a lovely time dancing with you, but... I have to go,' I said pointing at Clare, as if she was dragging me out, which she clearly wasn't.

'You're a great dancer,' he said giving me a kiss.

Well, I nearly floated off the podium back to Clare, who was asking for our tabs from the barman. I felt dead young and attractive, until the barman handed over the bills and Clare and I, in sync, put our glasses on so we could read the bloody things. I looked at Clare with her specs on a string round her neck. She looked at me. We both burst out laughing.

'We look like Hinge and Bracket,' I cried.

'Yeah, but how do you *feel*?' Clare grinned.

'Brill,' I said. 'Bloody brill.'

26

SHE'LL BE RUNNING DOWN THE MOUNTAIN WHEN SHE COMES

Mount Kilimanjaro is a dormant volcano in Tanzania. It is the highest mountain in Africa and the highest single free-standing mountain in the world at 5,895 metres above sea level.

Lesley, not surprisingly, told us we were 'one fucking sandwich short of a picnic' for going. 'Just the name alone sounds fucking terrifying. *Kill-a-man*?'

'Well, it's not *Kill-a-woman*, is it?' Clare said with a grin.

Lesley's husband Lee said he would love to go, joking that he wouldn't be the man the mountain kills. So Clare, ever the trooper, signed up, as did Judy another M2Ms girl, Suzanne, who had come to Vietnam and Cambodia with us, myself and Lee.

Lesley hadn't finished telling us how bonkers we were though. She googled the proof:

According to the Kilimanjaro Christian Medical Centre in Moshi, 25 people died from January 1996 to October 2003 while climbing the mountain. Seventeen were female and eight were male, ranging in age from 29 to 74. Fourteen died from advanced high altitude illness. The remaining eleven deaths resulted from trauma (3), myocardial infarction (4), pneumonia (2), cardio-pulmonary failure of other underlying cause (1), and acute appendicitis (1).

I knew there were dangers involved. Kilimanjaro doesn't involve ropes and crampons and all that specialist mountaineering gear. You can pretty much trek the whole way – people have even run up, which I thought was truly bonkers – but it's very cold at night, there are sometimes very high winds and, as Lesley pointed out, altitude sickness is a problem. A study of people attempting to reach the summit in July and August 2005 found that only sixty percent succeeded. So you have to acclimatise. We would do this, we were told, by taking the seven-day trek as opposed to the five-day one. If you take the five-day one you're more likely to get sick. Our seven-day one means we have time to come down the mountain a little bit each night to sleep, which is supposed to help with any sickness.

The rickety bus dropped us off at the base and we began our trek. There were about thirty in our group altogether. People from all walks of life, all areas of the UK, all ages. We hiked through woodland at first, much greener than I had expected as Moses and the rest of our Tanzanian guides shot off in their flip-flops and Manchester United T-shirts with Portaloos, chairs, tables and bags full of food on their backs.

'Christ. And we thought we were fit,' I said, watching them steam ahead.

'We have to sort out their clothes for them,' Clare said.

'Yeah, poor lads, they're going to be cold tonight, surely,' said Lee.

'Sod that,' Clare said. 'I mean, we have to swap those Manchester United shirts for Liverpool ones.'

Gradually the greenery fell away and things got a lot rockier and dustier. Even so, at the end of the first day hiking I was amazed to see our guides had a little village waiting for us. All our stuff was laid out on a tarpaulin for us to take to our little two-man tents which had somehow been put up on the rocky ground. There was even a table laid out with food – ginger biscuits were a big feature of every meal. I think the ginger was supposed to help with altitude sickness.

'Washey, washey!' called Moses.

And we needed that wash with hot water and Dettol soap. Not that we took our clothes off – there wasn't exactly a place to do that – but the dust got in every pore of your face and hands, the only bits that were uncovered. And then it was time to use the little Portaloo with the broken zip on its tent, so you had to hold it together as your head stuck out the top, looking at the majestic carpet of cloud below you as you balanced on a plastic throne that couldn't be further from majestic.

Each day to keep morale up we would sing as we trekked higher and higher, but as the days passed and the air thinned, we found we could barely speak a sentence, let alone sing. Before we flew to Tanzania, Clare and I had decided that hiking up and down Snowdonia twice in one day would be good training, but it seemed no matter how fit you were, or how much you trained, if the altitude sickness got you, you were done for.

It was only after a day or two that Lee got sick. The African doctor that accompanied our group told us Lee's blood pressure had started rising. He wouldn't give up, bless him, but he had to lag behind us quite a way. At every meal stop, he would have to find a place to lie down. We tried to get him to eat, but he couldn't keep it down.

'Are you going to eat that, Lee?' Clare said, hovering about, watching his plate like the hawks we'd seen scanning the mountainside for rodents.

He shook his head and she pounced on it.

'You've not lost your appetite, have you,' I laughed.

'A fly round shit, me, when it comes to food,' she said with her mouth full.

Day three or four, things got even more intense. The mountain was so steep in places we were scrambling on all fours at times and there were gaps in the trail that we needed to jump across with Moses and the others waiting on the other side to catch us and pull us to safety.

All thirty of us in the group got on famously. It didn't matter where we came from, or what we did in our lives back home – and we were so different; people you would never see together in the same place usually – we were all the same up here on this enormous mountain. As Clare said as we huddled in our little tent one night:

'Did you chat to that bloke who runs the ad agency?'

'Rupert?'

'Yeah.'

'What about him?' I asked thinking Clare might have the hots for him.

'I was just thinking, if he passed me in the streets of Liverpool in his suit he would say to himself, "Who's that scally?" but we get on like a house on fire here.'

Mother Nature didn't give a toss whether we were a banker or a shelf-stacker. We were all identical and insignificant dots to her on her turf.

I got chatting to another one of the group, a young lad called David, who didn't seem to have the right gear and was struggling with chafing.

'I would offer you some of my wicking fabric leggings, but I don't think they'd fit,' I smiled.

'It's OK,' he laughed. 'I wasn't supposed to be here, so I'm not really prepared.'

'What do you mean?'

'My mum signed up to do this last year. It was on her bucket list. But then she got cancer and...' He took a deep breath. 'She passed away.'

'Oh, love, I'm sorry,' I said. I felt that fist around my heart that I felt when my dad died. That was so many years ago, but I could still feel it. So I could imagine just how awful David would be feeling now.

He went on, 'So I'm going up for her.' He pulled a stone from his backpack, which he had painted white with a butterfly and the words: *The nearest I can get to you, Mum, in heaven.* 'I'm going to put it on the top.'

'That's brill. That's brill,' I said, rubbing his shoulders to comfort him though I was comforting myself just as much.

Day five was the day before we were to attempt the summit. We would only walk a short way that morning before lunch. After that, we were told to get some sleep. The guides would wake us for dinner and then encourage us to sleep some more before we started to climb at 11 p.m. in the hope that we would reach the summit for sunrise. But when they woke us to eat, I was so exhausted I refused to get up. Even the human dustbin Clare chose to stay sleeping rather than eat dinner, so she must have been shattered.

Though we chose to stay in bed, we were so apprehensive about the climb we could hardly sleep anyway, so we were up way before 11 p.m. chatting with Judy, Suzie and Lee, as far as we could chat in our constantly breathless state.

That was when the doctor came and told Lee that it was too dangerous in his condition to go to the summit.

'What?' he cried. 'I've come this far. I have to try.'

'If you try, you will die,' the doctor said. 'We cannot let you.'

Lee was gutted. And we were all gutted for Lee. We had a tearful hug before he waved us off. I don't think I would have kept it together if they had delivered that news to me. Luckily I had not had much more than a headache every day, which a couple of paracetamols seemed to sort out. And the rest of my girls were the same.

I looked up the mountainside. All I could see was blackness except for little strings of fairy lights here and there, which in fact were the head torches on the other groups of climbers already going up. I turned on my head torch too and began the slow shuffle into the darkness.

Perhaps an hour or so later – I was losing all sense of time – our guides stopped on a small plateau to feed us ginger tea. But before she could get some of that medicinal tea inside her, Judy threw up everywhere.

'I'm so sorry. So sorry,' she cried. 'I don't know where that came from. I'll be all right, I promise,' she told the doctor fearing he would give her the same news he'd given Lee.

Ken, our English group leader, came over and put his arm around her. 'Don't worry, don't worry. It happens to everyone.' And, as if to prove himself right, he immediately, out of nowhere, projectile vomited over Judy's shoulder.

'My God,' Clare whispered to me, trying not to laugh, 'what's happening?'

'I don't know,' I said, 'but I'm just glad I haven't honked.'

I took a sip of ginger tea, and then almost instantly, from the depth of my guts, liquid shot out of my mouth with as much force as the pea soup did from that poor girl in *The Exorcist*.

'Christ!' Clare squealed. 'Are you all right?'

'I'm fine,' I said. And I was. I didn't feel sick before I drank and I didn't feel sick now. 'I'm good to go.'

But Kilimanjaro hadn't finished with our group yet.

As we carried on climbing, Paul, a younger lad from London, started to complain of sight problems. He went blind in one eye. And then, as he examined Paul, our doctor went blind in one eye too. They both had to get themselves back down to where we'd started that night as quickly as possible to cure this condition known as snow blindness, which was brought on by the extreme altitude causing parts of the brain to swell and press on the nerves behind the eye.

Lee, Paul and now even our doctor. I hugged Judy, Suzie and Clare – proud of my girls, defying the stats that Lesley had googled about gender and surviving the mountain. It didn't surprise me though. These women, all the women I had met through M2Ms, were superheroes – having overcome mountains of one sort or another in their lives almost daily. They were far from the little women that Trevor, his father and the like thought should and could do nothing more than be seen and not heard.

We shuffled on. I wished I'd have been able to sleep after dinnertime because I was starting to feel knackered again. You know that feeling when you're driving on a boring straight motorway at one in the morning and you start to nod off? That's what I was experiencing now as I walked. In fact I think I actually walked for a while as I slept. It was all getting weirder and weirder by the minute. The weather had been really kind to us over the past five days, but we had never had to hike at night before. It was freezing, which made your body want to shut down even more.

When I saw a flat rock jutting from the side of the mountain, a cold and damp slab of stone, it was so inviting, as if it was upholstered in the softest velvet with pillows stuffed with eiderdown strewn all about. It looked like the perfect place to sit down.

'I've just got to stop here for a minute,' I called up ahead to the group.

'Do not sit down! Do not sit down! Not yet,' Moses called back and disappeared into the night.

Everyone was concentrating so hard on putting one foot in front of the other, they didn't notice me sneak back to the rock and sit. When my bum touched the stone I felt so relieved that I started dreaming of what it would be like to be snoozing in my tent right now. I envied Lee, Paul and the doctor so much I started to think of an excuse to go and join them. I racked my brains. 'What is a good enough reason for me to stop?' I asked myself. I so desperately wanted to give up that I was rifling through reasons I could give the others, reasons that would allow me to go back and still hold my head up, still be proud of how far I'd gone. But there was no excuse that would allow me to be proud if it wasn't the truth. If I didn't have ridiculously high blood pressure or hadn't gone blind, I had to keep going.

'Who says you have to keep going?' said the other part of me. And I got into a right big argument with myself about it. I was fighting and fighting and that's when I thought about Trevor and the kids and everything I have written in these pages here.

'You have to do this for the kids!' I told myself, looking up towards the dark mountain summit and the distant strings of fairy lights. 'You have to do it for the kids of Claire House. And you have to do it for Sam, Ben and Harriet. You can't give up now! Look what you've done, how far you've come! Show them what you can do when you put your mind to it! Show them they don't have to take his crap! And nor do I.'

And before the negative part of me could answer back, I felt a hand under my arm yanking me up.

'Come on, come on, keep going!' said a voice.

And so, with a combination of willpower and someone else's brute force, I did.

But as I gradually focused on the people around me I realised I knew none of them. It was a completely different group. It shouldn't have mattered. I mean, we were still heading to the summit. At least, I thought we were. And then I started to panic. What if this group is on the way down? What if they've already got to the top and are taking me back to camp, thinking I'd already been up there? 'Well, just ask them, you daft cow,' I told myself, but I could barely get a word out I was so short of breath.

Then I heard a wonderfully familiar and exotic voice. 'Rachel! Rachel!' It was Moses emerging from the darkness, linking arms with me and marching me up to join the rest of my group.

As I walked with Moses I realised I could see much more of him than I could when he had told me not to sit down God knows how many minutes or hours ago. I turned off my head torch. I have no idea when it happened, but the sky had started to get lighter, turning every stunning hue of pink, orange and blue you could imagine.

'You made it,' he said.

'You what?' I said.

I looked about me. I saw Clare, Suzie, Judy. We were at the summit. The sun exploded in slow motion through the clouds and we all danced around hugging each other as if we ran on solar panels and were instantly and fully recharged. We stood there, taking in this out-of-this-world sight, a sight we might never see again. The closest thing to heaven.

I turned around and through my tearful eyes I spotted David sitting away from the group looking out over some awesomely humungous glaciers, which were a shade of turquoise I had never seen anywhere else. I gave him a minute then went over. The stone with the butterfly on it was on the ground by his side.

'You OK, love?'

He nodded, his eyes as full as mine.

I put a hand on his shoulder. 'You've done it. You've bloody done it. She's so proud of you right now. She knows, you know.'

'Thanks, Rachel.'

'I hope my kids are as wonderful as you when they get to your age,' I said, telling myself that they would be, as long as their hearts weren't crushed by their father's emotional constipation.

It was time to go down far too soon. It would only take a few hours to walk down, but it would take half that time if you…

'…run!' beamed Moses. 'Who wants to run down?'

'Run?' said Clare. 'How the hell do you run down that?' She peered down at the route Moses was pointing out which looked like a ski slope without any snow.

'Fast,' Moses grinned.

Run down Kilimanjaro? It was totally bonkers, but I couldn't think of a better way to end this epic journey. Running is what I do. It's what I've always done, for better or worse. Racing through life after waking up from those night terrors as a little girl, scared I wouldn't achieve anything before I died. Running from the bullies. Running to auditions, running through airports, down hospital corridors, running from a psychotic Japanese husband, from a controlling English one, running to Zumba classes, running half marathons, full marathons, up enormous sand dunes in the Sahara, across south-east Asian countries, and running into other women that would save my life as much as they reckoned I saved theirs.

So of course I was going to run down this mountain, however nuts it seemed.

Moses handed me a hiking stick and told me to link arms with him. Judy was up for it too and linked arms with another guide, who also handed her a stick, which, they told us, would help us balance. You know the sticks I mean, like you use in skiing. Well, it turned out we did virtually ski down this dusty mountainside. We flew down with the help of gravity and our guides, slipping over, laughing deliriously and ending up covered in the soot we'd kicked up, the inside of our mouths coated with it. I marvelled at how quick and easy it seemed after being so slow and hard to get to the top. We were back at the camp and reunited with Lee within a couple of hours. And by the end of the day we were back at the base we had left five days ago, no altitude sickness slowing us down.

It's incredible what you can do when Mother Nature is on your side. And if she's not – say, she doesn't give you the right chemicals in your brain to keep you out of depression for very long – then you have to find another way to get to the top of the mountains you face. Listen to the guides who come out of the darkness to suggest a route, listen to the voice inside you, the one that sounds like you, not the one that hisses like a controlling spouse, but most of all reach out to others, find your own version of Mums to Marathons. And I'm not suggesting you lead a club or run a marathon – although I would say, run. Even if it's just for a few minutes at first. Sometimes I know that just stepping out of the front door can seem an impossible task, but, as they say, a journey of a thousand miles starts with a single step. One small step for woman, one giant leap for your mental health. No excuses. You can't find your water bottle? Use your two-year-old's Peppa Pig one. Don't have a Tubigrip for your knee? Cut the toes off your hubby's Hugo Boss sock to make one. He won't mind, honest. Can't run? I would beg to differ. In fact I'll prove it if you come and see me. Get in touch! But if you can't do that, then walk, but whatever you do get over the doorstep. That's an achievement. If you don't do a mile, don't beat yourself up, be kind to yourself. Next time you will. You can't win the lottery unless you buy a ticket. You can't get better unless you take that first step. So put your trainers on! Go on! Buy a ticket! And for God's sake reach out to friends for support. You'll be surprised how quickly they'll jump at the chance to help you to the mountaintop, because without a shadow of a doubt, I guarantee they've been trying to get to the top themselves for one reason or another. You're not the only one fumbling through the freezing night. You can help them as much as they can you, and when that sinks in, no matter how thin the air can feel, how hard it might be to breathe sometimes, together you'll reach the summit and bask in the sunlight of a new day.

27

THIS IS ME

Trevor asked me to meet him at a café next to his shop, not far from Bebington in a little courtyard of beautiful boutiques, embroidery shops, a hat shop, an ice cream parlour and a bistro. The last place I'd associate with Trevor. The sun was shining and it was warm enough to have our coffees outside.

It had been more than a month since Sam had had enough of his dad and decided to live full time with me. Trevor never got it that, like me, the kids would prefer a genuine hug to a genuine Tommy Hilfiger top any day.

'We don't have to change anything officially with Child Support yet,' Trevor said, tearing the corner off a napkin. 'Sam'll come crawling back soon and then we'll have to change it back again. It's not worth the hassle.'

Not worth the hassle? There he went trying to control me again. And I wasn't going to be controlled anymore. I'd conquered Mount Kilimanjaro, for God's sake, I wasn't going to let this little man defeat me.

I sighed. Gulped down a large mouthful of coffee and gently stood up. 'Goodbye, Trevor,' I said softly and walked away.

*

That same year, 2019, at the age of fifty I was diagnosed with ADHD. It wasn't a surprise to many people, especially my colleagues at the Involve Northwest office where I worked. I was fine going out and about, meeting clients and giving them help, but when it came to inputting data back at the office I couldn't focus. One of my colleagues asked me, half joking, if I'd ever been tested for ADHD and when my manager overheard this he said, 'Our Rachel doesn't need a test to know she's got ADHD, of course she has.'

'Really?' I said. 'Do you think so?'

My manager could see I was anxious to know for sure so he arranged for the company to send me for a test at a private clinic in Liverpool.

They stuck this thing on my head like Doc Brown from *Back to the Future* might wear and made me do all sorts of tests on a computer while they measured my brainwaves. A score over 84 would mean I had ADHD. I scored 98.

'Well, that's pretty definitive,' I thought, but the clinician had other ideas.

'We can't be sure,' he said, 'because you're not relaxed enough to do the test. You're too hyperactive right now.'

I didn't want to be rude but wasn't that the bloody definition of ADHD? 'This is me. All the time,' I explained.

They asked me to come back, but I didn't want my workplace throwing good money after bad with these numbskulls. So I went to my GP and had a test there.

'I don't know how you've coped all these years,' she said scanning the results with her eyebrows creeping up and up her forehead as she read them.

But I'd realised by now that it was the ADHD that drove me to keep doing the next thing. Yes, it led me down some dark alleys and fooled me into making some bad decisions, but it drove me to dance, it drove me to work hard, it drove me to run marathons, trek deserts, cycle through continents and climb mountains, both real and metaphorical, it led me to my sisters, my community, my saviours. And without those things and those people in my life, no, I wouldn't have coped.

'That's who I am. This ADHD is me,' I told the doctor. 'If I had had it suppressed by drugs when I was younger, I might never have done all these things that have made me so happy. I might never have met all the wonderful people that have shown me such support.'

It was appropriate then, that almost to the day of my ADHD diagnosis, Mums to Marathons became a Community Interest Company, which is basically a special form of non-charitable non-profit limited company, which exists primarily to benefit a community or pursue a social purpose. As the full-time director of this CIC, I would be paid for leading new groups of runners and we would also be given that desperately needed funding to pay for more leaders, like our Lynne and Clare, to take other groups so I wasn't stretched to breaking point again as M2Ms continued to grow.

There were so many women running now in Bebington alone that sometimes they formed little groups of their own and decided that they would rather run when it suited them and where it suited them, outside of the M2Ms club. I have to admit, this really wound me up at first. I took it personally. I was offended that they thought they could do better on their own. After all, for me, Mums to Marathons was always about community, being stronger together and all that. When I moaned to Lesley about it she got ready to go out and 'tear them a new one.' I loved her for her protectiveness, but I also loved the way her explosive reaction put my own thoughts into perspective and I realised, if I didn't want to be laid up in hospital with pneumonia again, or something worse, all these women running in their own little groups was a gift.

I would see groups of runners all over town that had never existed before. Bebington was like the Stepford for runners. But instead of getting upset about it now I was simply proud that all these women (and some men) were running because of Mums to Marathons, whether they still ran with us or not.

I'll be driving in the car somewhere and the kids will point out the window and say, 'Mum, are they one of yours?'

'Yeah,' I'll say.

Or:

'They used to be,' and I beam with pride. 'But now it looks like they've found their own way. And that's just fab, isn't it.'

I'll look at my kids in the rear-view mirror. They'll nod and watch the runners go.

One day soon our Sam, Ben and Harriet will fly the nest just like some of my M2Ms girls have done. And I'll be as proud of them as I am of my runners for doing it. God knows how it will bend my head when my children find their own way in life, when they leave home, leaving me with empty-nest syndrome to add to the mix of my mental health, but it's OK, I'm ready, I'm tooled up, I'm armed to the teeth now. I've got the Orange Army to protect me. I've got my sisters to link arms with on the steep slopes of life. And I've got the greatest and simplest weapon of all: my trainers, waiting by the front door for when the time comes. And, my God, how many marathons I'll do then!

EPILOGUE

Me and Lesley were having a girls' night in watching Netflix with a bottle of Prosecco. Well, Netflix was on but we were talking way too much to pay attention to the film, apart from the scenes that Jason Momoa was in of course.

'Ooh, if I was ten years younger and a few inches tighter.'

'Les!' I screamed as if I wasn't thinking the same thing.

She giggled into her glass, then said, 'Why don't you get out there and meet someone new, Rach?'

I sighed. 'How am I going to meet anyone else at my age?'

'Ah-ha!' she said. 'Give me your phone!'

'Why?'

'Just give it here!' She snatched it and began to download an app. 'All the kids are doing it these days. They don't have to go out clubbing or whatever to meet anyone. You can do it all on this.'

'What's that?'

'It's called Tinder. Look! You put in a few details about yourself, a few pics, then you swipe.'

'Swipe what?'

In no time Lesley had my profile up and running and she was demonstrating exactly how to swipe. 'Nah... nah... nobhead... nah... definitely not... too hairy... too short... too ugly... too nerdy... Now, he's a bit of alright, we'll have him...'

'Hang on!' I grabbed the phone. 'Shouldn't I be the one deciding who's a bit of alright and who's not?'

'Well, get on with it, mate, before you dry up for good down there.'

We had a laugh swiping left and right for half an hour, but I soon got bored. It didn't seem real anyway. I felt like I was just playing some kind of video game.

A day or two later I was out in Birkenhead Park walking our dog Flo. I'd bought her a couple of years after leaving Trevor. She's a chihuahua, looks like a rat in a posh coat, but we love her to bits.

I stopped to rest her little legs and sat on a bench looking out over the lake at all the trees beyond turning red and yellow against a bright blue sky. Then this bloke sat down at the other end of the bench and, me being me, I started chatting. Quirky looking fella he was, sports jacket, scarf, long tousled hair. Arty type I thought. A bit of alright really. I introduced him to Flo. He made a joke. I laughed. So did he.

'Life's too short not to laugh at least once a day, I reckon,' he said.

'God, that sounds good to me,' I said.

'Rachel, isn't it?' he smiled.

'How did you know?' I said, turning towards him and examining his face more closely now.

He was about my age, but it only took a second before I recognised the seventeen-year-old boy who used to run the Port Sunlight Players.

'Brian McCann?'

He nodded.

'Brian bloody McCann. What are you doing here?'

'I never went away. But I hear you did.'

'For a while yeah,' I said looking out at the autumn trees. 'But I'm back now.'

'That's good,' he smiled.

'Yeah?'

'Yeah.'

I edged a bit closer to him. 'Do you remember that time in the Port Sunlight Players when I had to kiss Andy whatshisname?'

'I do. I…' He cleared his throat and edged a bit closer too, '…wished it was me.'

'You what?'

He blushed.

'You fancied me?' I said gobsmacked that a clever creative type like him would even give me a second look. 'Then why did you send us off to another room to practise, like?'

'I didn't want to ruin the play either.'

'Oh my God, you were dead serious about the theatre, weren't you?' I said, shifting along the bench a bit more.

'Still am. Do you still dance?' He slid a bit further towards me too.

'Nah, do I look like a dancer?'

'You look great.' He blushed again.

So did I. 'Well, I run a lot. I have a club actually. I try to help other women, you know.'

'That's great,' he said.

'Still writing songs and plays and that?' I asked.

'Yes. Made a bit of a career out of it. I do a lot in schools these days. Try to help kids, you know.'

By this time we were right next to each other on the bench, staring into each other's faces like we were looking in the mirror.

'Oh really? That's fab. Remember this one? *I'm Santa Claus as everyone knows, a fat man with a beard. I'm dressed in red, silly hat on my head, but no one thinks I'm weird.* Yeah I know, still no Bette Midler, but…' I stopped jabbering on as he looked like he'd seen a ghost. 'You OK?'

'Yes, yes, I'm great. It's just… that song. How did you remember that?'

'I used to sing it to my kids. Harriet my little'un knows it off by heart.'

'Really?' He looked like he might well up. 'That's amazing.'

'Brian, you have no idea. That song helped stop me from going nuts on a few occasions, I can tell you.'

'How many kids do you have?'

'Three.'

'Married then?' He shrunk back into himself a bit and looked at the grass.

'Nope. Happily divorced.' He looked up and I said, 'So do you still fancy me or what?'

He laughed and relaxed again.

We must have chatted for a couple of hours before I had to go. We walked back to the car park together.

'That's my car there,' I said.

'This is mine,' he said sauntering to a great big gorgeous-looking Jaguar. He pointed his key ring at it and pressed the button to unlock it, but it was the dumpy little car behind it that responded, beeping like our Flo barking. 'Oh,' he pretended to be embarrassed. 'I suppose that must be mine then.'

I cracked up.

'So shall we meet up again?' he smiled.

'What do you mean, a date, like?'

'Yes, if you want to, but…'

'Who needs bloody Tinder,' I giggled to myself.

'What was that?'

'I said, yeah. Yeah I want to. I'd bloody love to actually.'

Brian is still making me smile every day. He makes us all smile. There is never a stern or sombre face in the house when Brian is around. I didn't know it was possible to have a partner who could make me feel so special, who tells me I'm beautiful even when I know I'm not – not because he's fibbing, but because that's genuinely how he sees me, and he's made me secure enough to know that's the truth. It couldn't be more of a contrast to those dark days before.

My little girl Harriet said to me just the other day, 'Mummy, when Brian is around everything seems lighter. He doesn't even have to speak either, it just feels better when he's here.'

That says it all. I know the boys feel the same because they've told me. And so do I.

I have found my forever and it feels fab.

GLOSSARY

Just like Keels learnt a new lingo when she became a prison officer, some of the words and phrases used on Merseyside may be new to you. Here's what they mean:

a bit of a cob on	rather irritated
boss	very good indeed
disco biscuits	ecstasy pills
divvy	a stupid person
doolally	crazy
jib	to give up
kecks	trousers
Mackie's	McDonald's
ozzie	hospital
scally	an irresponsible, roguish person
scouser	a person from Liverpool
tear them a new one	tell someone off furiously
wools	persons from the Wirral
yers	you

ACKNOWLEDGEMENTS

Rachel

Firstly, I would like to acknowledge and thank my amazing school teacher Sylvia Reed. Sylvia has believed in me since I was eleven years old to the present day. Everyone needs a teacher like this. She made me believe in myself when other teachers didn't. I will always be grateful to her for the encouragement she gave me, for her interest and belief in me. Thank you, Sylvia.

To Clare Finlay, Lesley Nilsson Perry, Melissa Fletcher, Keels Warke and Helen Byrne for spilling your beans to Warren. You all amaze me, my sisters from other misters.

To Mark who has always gone above and beyond the call of duty as my accountant. He introduced me to many people who have opened many doors for me. He has also tried to help me become more organised but to no avail. For this, Mark, I am sorry, but thanks for not giving up on me.

I want to acknowledge Warren FitzGerald who took me and my story on. He believed in me even though, during times of my waffling, his ears must have bled. This book would not have happened without him. Thank you, Warren.

To my hero, my dad, Derek Brown who died in 1989. Never a day goes by that I don't think about you and what you would say to me about my mad adventures. I know you'll be smiling.

To my amazingly wonderful mum Joan Brown, who has always been there for me no matter what. There must have been many times you wanted to cry with all my dramas, my ups and downs, but instead you envelope me in your arms and tell me not to worry, everything's going to be OK.

To my beautiful sister Lynney, who has had horrendous trials to bear of her own but is still always there for me. She worries about me constantly and always checks in to make sure I'm OK. Lynney, I love you to the moon and back.

To my brother (in law) Lewi (Steve), who stands beside my sister and adores her – for that I love and adore you, Lewi.

To my Auntie Liney (Irene Bomber), who I have always considered to be a very wise lady – she also pours a great gin. You are like another mum to me, Auntie Liney, and like a second nan to my kids, spoiling them rotten.

To my other half Brian McCann, who understands my mad days, my real madness, and yet asks no questions – he already knows.

Finally, to the loves of my life: my three outstandingly fantastic children, Sam, Ben and Harriet, who I couldn't be more proud of. Your love is all I need.

Warren

I want to thank you, Rachel, for trusting me with your story. In a world increasingly concerned with dividing people, I am grateful to have stories like yours to tell; stories of coming together, of bonding, of unity. In a time of incredible loss for me personally and for the entire population of the world, your inspiring and irrepressible spirit has kept me going.

Thanks to all the Mums to Marathons family who have contributed in some way to this book, especially Lynne, Keels, Lesley, Melissa, Clare, and Helen, for adding your vivid voices to the picture.

Thanks to John Blake for not hesitating to get behind this book – nice to be working with you again. Thanks to Rob, Jon and all the team at Ad Lib.

Thanks to family and friends for love and support, particularly Matt, Sheila and Kenai Hart for being… my rock doesn't seem sufficient. How about: my Uluru? Sarah and Ian Golding for being there despite any distance. Steve Jones for your boundless enthusiasm, brainstorming and support.

Thank you Gayan Perera for unconditional love. I know you'd be proud and I thank you for making sure I know. I dedicate my work here about an inspirational woman to my very own inspiration. You will always be 'mage pani'.

www.mumstomarathons.org.uk

ABOUT THE AUTHORS

Rachel Brown was born in Bromborough and grew up in Spital, Bebington on the Wirral Peninsula.

Blessed with a happy childhood and close family, she attended Stanton Road Primary School and Bebington Secondary School For Girls before becoming a professional dancer, working with dance troupes all over the world for seven years.

Rachel now lives back in Bromborough with her three children Sam, Ben and Harriet. She is happily partnered to playwright and composer Brian McCann.

Warren FitzGerald was born in 1973 in Hertfordshire. He is an author and screenwriter.

His debut novel *The Go-Away Bird* won an Amazon Rising Stars Award, was longlisted for the Authors' Club Best First Novel Award and was Waterstones' Book of the Month in October 2011.

His first non-fiction book *All in the Same Boat* (published in 2016), has been optioned for the screen with Warren himself co-writing the screenplay adaptation.

Breaking Dad (a memoir written in collaboration with the subject James Lubbock) was published in 2019. It too has been optioned for the screen.